eXtreme Programming in Action

eXtreme Programming in Action

Practical experiences from real world projects

**Martin Lippert, Stefan Roock,
Henning Wolf**

JOHN WILEY & SONS, LTD

Telephone (+44) 1243 779777
e-mail (for orders and customer service enquiries): cs-books@wiley.co.uk
Visit our Home Page on http://www.wileyeurope.com or www.wiley.com

Other Wiley Editorial Offices

John Wiley & Sons Inc., 111 River Street, Hoboken, NJ 07030, USA

Jossey-Bass, 989 Market Street, San Francisco, CA 94103-1741, USA

Wiley-VCH Verlag GmbH, Boschstr. 12, D-69469 Weinheim, Germany

John Wiley & Sons Australia Ltd, 33 Park Road, Milton, Queensland 4064, Australia

John Wiley & Sons (Asia) Pte Ltd, 2 Clementi Loop #02-01, Jin Xing Distripark, Singapore 129809

John Wiley & Sons Canada Ltd, 22 Worchester Road, Etobicoke, Ontario, Canada M9W 1L1

Library of Congress Cataloguing in Publication Data

(to follow)

British Library Cataloguing in Publication Data

A catalogue record for this book is available from the British Library

ISBN 0 470 84705 0

Translated and typeset by Cybertechnics Ltd, Sheffield
Printed and bound in Great Britain by Biddles Ltd, Guildford and King's Lynn
This book is printed on acid-free paper responsibly manufactured from sustainable forestry, in which at least two trees are planted for each one used for paper production.

Contents

Preface

- Can software be developed more quickly?

- Do current development processes produce high-quality software?

- Is the risk of failure higher than in other development disciplines?

These questions fan a heated debate about *Extreme Programming (XP)*. Whilst these questions defy definite answers, our experience with XP provides some food for thought. We hope that the way we present our experience in this book can help your practice.

XP is a provocative development method that has come to the attention of programmers over the last few years. It has grabbed their attention as they strive for a slimmer, more lightweight and agile development process. In such an environment, a development method must have a clear justification for everything that it incorporates. In some cases, this striving may go too far, but XP has brought a breath of fresh air to the discussion on development methods.

Kent Beck published the first book on XP but he did not develop it alone. A number of his colleagues started to use XP and a community has grown up around it. Ron Jeffries, Martin Fowler and Robert C. Martin are prominent members of this community who have published books on XP. Since 2000, Europe has hosted an annual International Conference on eXtreme Programming and Agile Processes in Software Engineering.[1] The US conference for Extreme Programming is XP/Agile Universe.[2]

Background　　Since the beginning of 1999,[3] we have used XP techniques to develop applications in a number of successful, commercial projects, as well as for the development of frameworks (Chapter 8 describes some of these projects). We know that XP has considerable potential in developing high-quality software. Our motivation for writing this book is to describe our experiences and thus help other software developers to use XP successfully in their projects.

---

1. The short title of the conference is XP2002, XP2003, and so on (see http://www.xp2002.org). XP2000 was the first conference on XP.

---

2. See http://xpuniverse.com/home.

---

3. How could we use XP techniques at the start of 1999, before the publication of Kent Beck's book? Many of the techniques had been discussed for years before that. Ward Cunningham discussed many XP techniques, including pair programming, in 'EPISODES: A pattern language of competitive development' (in John M. Vlissides, James O. Coplien, Norman L. Kerth, *Pattern Languages of Program Design 2*, Addison-Wesley, 1996). Furthermore, in April 1999, we took part in an extreme programming workshop led by Kent Beck.

Thanks   Over these last years, we have discussed XP experiences and concepts with far too many people to name individually. We would therefore like to thank those with whom we have had particularly intensive discussions:

- The experiences of the members of the German language XP mailing list (xp-forum@egroups.com) have given us new perspectives and ways of working.

- Throughout Germany there are XP user groups that meet more or less regularly. We have had valuable discussions at the XP user group in Hamburg (xpug-hh@yahoogroups.com), which meets about once a month.

- We have had interesting conversations at various conferences with Frank Westphal, Christian Wege and Hans Wegener.

- We have had a number of articles published at the XP 2000 and XP 2001 conferences and have had important feedback from both the reviewers and participants at the conference. We would particularly like to thank the participants and organisations of the 'Experience Exchange' workshop at XP 2001.

- Alex Bepple, Tammo Freese, Dierk König, Johannes Link, Marko Schulz and Frank Westphal read early versions of this book and gave us detailed and constructive feedback.

- We come from the tradition of WAM, which means that we have tried to combine positive experiences from both WAM and XP.[4] In the process, those with whom we share the WAM background have supported us: Heinz Züllighoven, Guido Gryczan, Karl-Heinz Sylla, Carola Lilienthal, Wolf-Gideon Bleek, Holger Bohlmann, Holger Breitling and many others.

---

4. WAM is a German acronym that stands for 'Werkzeug, Automat, Material'. In English, we translate it as 'tools and materials metaphor'. The method contains metaphors and both conceptual and implementation frameworks. However, this does not mean that we are trying to sell WAM under the label of XP. This book presents our experiences with XP, not with WAM.

- Since 2000, we have been working as consultants and developers at IT Workplace Solutions. We have been able to benefit from talking to more than 30 of our colleagues about our experience.

- At IT Workplace Solutions, we have carried out a number of development projects. The experience presented in this book was gained by working on these projects. Credit is due to our project partners and our colleagues for their highly productive cooperation.

- We have also worked as scientific assistants in the area of software technology at the Faculty of Computer Science at the University of Hamburg. Our colleagues in the software engineering department have vigorously supported our work and have given us the opportunity to pick out XP as a central theme in seminars and practical work.

- Within the scope of the work at IT Workplace Solutions, we occasionally spent substantial time in hotel rooms. One of the authors spent the whole of 2001 in a small town in Germany with a customer. We thank the town fathers for the lack of glamorous distractions in the town, which meant that there was enough time to write this book.

- Last but not least, we give thanks to our wives, for more than we can disclose here.

Martin Lippert
Stefan Roock
Henning Wolf

Foreword

In the Foreword to *Planning Extreme Programming*, by Beck and Fowler Tom DeMarco explains that the principles of XP are means to make process irrelevant. What does he mean by that?

Each team and each project is unique and therefore needs its own custom-made process. In fact, a process wants to be adapted to the locale and be continuously improved. That requires constant reflection and reorientation. The development process is developing itself through its own development process. That's why it's important to be aware of it. How does XP help you?

Extreme Programming describes a value system as well as a bunch of generative principles, and recommends a system of practices that support each other in the highest degree. These practices are really only the starting line – they don't actually represent XP just yet, although they should eventually lead to it. The finish is to apply XP practices until they've become entirely second nature, and to evolve our own process based on this foundation. How is this supposed to work?

Regularly holding a retrospective can help continuously improve the development process and to avoid making the same mistake twice. Frankly, you wouldn't practice XP, if you didn't change your process from iteration to iteration. Constant learning is an unwritten value in Extreme Programming and short iterations in particular allow experimentation with the process itself.

Martin, Stefan and Henning speak from their own hands-on experience. They successfully completed several projects, aiming to come as close to the XP ideals as possible. They didn't blindly follow some dogma. Instead they've periodically reflected upon their work. What worked well? What didn't? What are areas for improvement? What have we learned that we don't want to forget? This way, they've come across some useful adaptations. I'm sure that the discussion of these techniques will prove a valuable asset to your own tool box. Either the techniques will work right away as described, or you'll have to make them fit your current situation. Just experiment. Play with your process!

Frank Westphal
Independent trainer and consultant
Hamburg, September 2002

Introduction

1.1   The values of XP

Four values XP is based on four values: simplicity, feedback, communication and courage. These values are important keys to XP. Anyone who can adopt these values can learn the practices and implement XP successfully. Those who cannot identify with these values will not find XP practices much help.

Simplicity XP aims to find the simplest solutions possible: *the simplest thing that could possibly work*. Simple solutions are quicker and more cost effective to produce than complex ones. They are also easier to explain, maintain, and develop. Simplicity incidentally refers to the development process. Therefore, XP itself is kept simple.

Feedback Quality control is important to every software development project. In an XP project, quality is ensured by means of *feedback*. The feedback takes place at different levels: for example, developers receive feedback about the correctness of their software from unit tests and users give feedback about wether the software is helpful.

Communication All members of the project team should *communicate* intensively. Special importance is given to personal conversation, since information is exchanged more effectively this way. In particular, misunderstandings and ambiguities can be ironed out immediately. If intensive communication between the members of the project is guaranteed, a good part of the otherwise normal documentation can be done away with. For various reasons, written documentation can still be useful or necessary (for example, revision security in banks and insurance companies). However, this documentation is not a deciding factor for the success of the project.

Courage Simple solutions, feedback and communication require *courage*, particularly if you are not used to dealing with these values. Simple solutions require courage because they can expose the fact that the solution was too simple. Developers need to be sure that their software is well-structured so that later requirements can be implemented easily. Developers sometimes think – consciously or unconsciously – that they are infallible and do not like to be criticised about the software they have developed. Communication requires courage because it can expose errors and show up things that have to be changed in the software. During the communication between users and customers, developers must get to know the domain language. They must leave the cosy environment of technology, with which they are familiar, and learn to cope with uncertainty in the application domain.

Finally, developers must communicate with the management hierarchy in order to introduce XP into a company.

Whether we are talking about an XP project or about extreme programming in general, we are always talking about the people that are involved. From the values, it is clear the people taking part in the project are the focal point, rather than tools, processes or the product.

1.2 The principles of XP

The principles of XP are derived from the values of XP. The five central principles are *Rapid Feedback, Assume Simplicity, Incremental Change, Embrace Change* and *Quality Work*. The other principles are *Teach Learning, Small Initial Investment, Play to Win, Concrete Experiments, Open and Honest Communication, Work with People's Instincts Not Against Them, Accept Responsibility, Local Adaptations, Travel Light,* and *Honest Measurement.*

Rapid Feedback:

Feedback should be obtained as quickly as possible. From the psychology of learning, we know that the amount of time between action and feedback plays an important part in the success of learning. The less time the greater the success. We will also avoid the risk of thinking and working in the wrong direction for an unnecessary length of time.

Assume Simplicity:

Simple solutions have a number of important advantages over complicated solutions. They are quicker to create, which means that we can get feedback earlier, and easier to understand and communicate. Simple solutions can also be modified more quickly, which is why we can react more flexibly to data that changes during the development process. Initially, the assumption of simplicity caused many software developers problems, since we were taught to plan for the future. It may appear paradoxical, but simple solutions are the best way to prepare for the future. Since we have no idea what the future has in store for us, it is more efficient not to speculate about it. Because our simple solutions are easy to change, we are ready to implement any possible requirement that the future throws at us.

Incremental Change:

Even if we assume simplicity, software systems in the process of development are so complex that changes can cause unexpected effects. Only if we always undertake small changes do these effects remain controllable. If we make large changes, there is a very high risk of side effects that cannot be controlled. If a number of changes induce side effects, we cannot establish how they are related to each other.

Embrace Change:

Simple solutions have to change to fulfil requirements that come up later. This approach to software development can only work if developers understand that changes to requirements, to parts of systems, and to development processes are not undesirable. Developers need to understand that all changes have a positive effect on the development project. They must not be reluctant to implement the necessary changes and must, in fact, *welcome* them.

Quality Work:

No developer wants to write poor software. Developers who produce high-quality software have increased job satisfaction and productivity, but it must be clear who decides the quality. Sometimes, software developers confuse their own standards of quality with those of the user. The user must define at least the standard for the 'quality of use' of the software. Direct feedback from the user allows the quality of use to be evaluated as frequently as possible and also helps developers to produce successful results.

Teach Learning:

Sometimes, XP is dogmatically imposed by its supporters. However, XP has precisely the opposite philosophy: it wants to teach developers in order that they may learn. Developers should themselves learn how many tests are required, rather than being asked to create a certain number of tests.

Small Initial Investment:

Software development projects often run over time and over budget. In order to minimise financial losses, the initial investment should be as low as possible. This means that the developer and user have to operate within a careful financial framework and concentrate on the most important aspects of the project. In the past, some projects were carried out with very large budgets and financial freedom. Most of these ended in disaster.

Play to Win:

In an XP project, which plays to win, the project team is concerned with the tasks on hand. In a traditional project, which often plays not to lose, the project team is concerned with not making errors. The XP team is clearly at an advantage: although they make errors, they will learn from their mistakes and grow into their tasks. This principle is also concerned with not wasting resources on dead projects. If nothing more can be gained, we should clearly admit it and terminate the project.

Concrete Experiments:

Every time we make a decision, it could be the wrong one. In order to minimise risks, we try to attain clarity as quickly as possible. Selective experiments can help achieve this clarity: tests of software systems can establish whether a design decision was suitable; reviews of the development process can determine whether other decisions were right or wrong.

Open and Honest Communication:

This principle is a truism. Fears, conceit and rivalry are often responsible for the failure of development projects. Therefore, establishing open and honest communication is a central and very demanding task.

Work with People's Instincts, Not Against Them:

This principle is difficult to implement in practice, since 'instinct' and 'semi-skilled behaviour' are hard to separate. Even in traditional projects, developers often work in pairs on a particularly complex problem. However, in inexperienced XP teams, pair programming is often forsaken under time pressure. Is this instinctive behaviour? Or do the developers go back to their semi-skilled way of behaving? However, a reasonable measure is that if the whole team thinks that something is nonsense, it may actually be nonsense. In other words, we should go with the saying 'What sounds like rubbish often is rubbish'.

Accept Responsibility:

Responsibility should not be assigned, but taken. If a project team is assigned the responsibility for a difficult project, it may have catastrophic effects on the motivation of the team and, therefore, on the results of the project. If the team takes the responsibility, the developers will own and feel responsible for their tasks. This improves motivation within the team and the chance of success of the project.

Local Adaptations:

It is highly unlikely that your project can use XP in the exact form that is described by Kent Beck ([Beck 00]). The aim is to complete the project successfully, not to reproduce the XP method exactly. Every adaptation of XP that supports this aim is justified.

Travel Light:

You cannot move forward quickly with heavy baggage and must select the 'marching pack' carefully. This is true for software development: you need a software development method and a few simple tools and frameworks that can be combined flexibly.

Honest Measurement:

In order to keep the development process under control, measurements must be made. However, they only make sense if the team measures things honestly. Successful tests look very good. But if they are only successful because the developers deleted all the parts that do not work, the measurements are no longer meaningful. They can even have negative effects on the project because they suggest a certainty that does not exist.

1.3 The practices of XP

The values and principles of XP are supported by practices (see Fig. 1.1) that help the developer to keep faithful to the principles. Fig. 1.1 is complex because of the connections between practices that influence each other. When adapting XP to local conditions, it is important to understand the network of connections between the practices, in order to avoid unde sirable side effects.

An important prerequisite for the effectiveness of XP practices is a flat cost of change curve (see Fig. 1.2). Traditional development processes frequently assume a steep cost of change curve: the production of a requirement gets exponentially more expensive with time. This means that it is vitally important to analyse completely all requests. XP, on the other hand, assumes that the implementation cost of a request is fixed, which removes the need to know all the requirements at the start of the project. For this reason, XP always concentrates on the current tasks.

Whether this flat cost of change curve can actually be achieved in a project depends on the technologies that are being used.

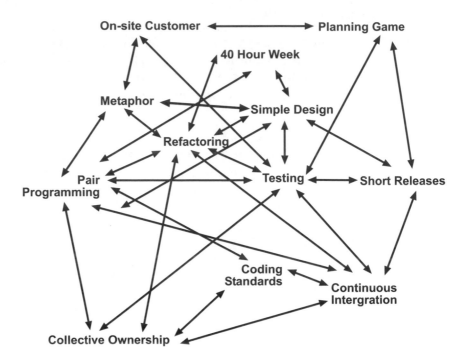

Figure 1.1 The connections between XP practices (see [Beck 00])

Traditional imperative programming languages often lead to steep cost of change curves, whilst object-oriented technologies potentially allow flat cost of change curves.

If the cost of change curve is not flat, many XP practicespractices (for example, *refactoring*, *simple design*, *small releases*, and *continuous integration*) cannot be implemented because they rely on the assumption that it always costs the same to make any particular change. Although object-oriented technologies can achieve a flat cost of change curve, they have to be used in an appropriate way. In particular, core abstractions of the application should be implemented only once in clearly comprehensible system components (the 'Once-And-Only-Once' principle).

On-site customer   XP projects always include both the user and the customer who provide the technical requirements for the project (see Section 2.1). Developers do not get a specification[1] from the user or customer, who is available to the developers and can be questioned at any time.

1. That is, there are no conventional documents such as system specifications that completely describe the system. Acceptance tests (see Section 2.5) take on part of the role of the specification.

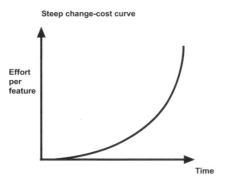

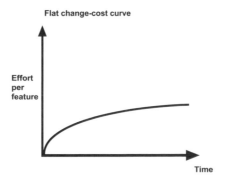

Figure 1.2 Steep vs. flat cost of change curves

Planning game XP projects run cyclically and incrementally. The extent of an increment is determined by the user, customer and developer in the planning game (see Section 2.2). The user and customer prioritise the requirements and the developers are responsible for estimating the cost.

Metaphors XP systems follow clear *metaphors* (see Section 2.3) that describe the core ideas and support the ongoing development of the system.

Small releases XP projects make new and modified system components available to the user within short periods of time (see Section 2.4). The user and customer can quickly evaluate and profit from the system. The evaluation can affect further development.

Testing Everything that has been programmed should be tested for quality control (see Section 2.5). Individual system components are tested by unit tests that can be automatically executed and technical requirements are checked by acceptance tests. The final acceptance test takes place when the system is used by the user.

Simple design   The software system should be designed as simple as possible (see Section 2.6). Simple designs can be implemented more easily and more quickly. They are also easier to understand, faster to communicate, and easier to test.

Refactoring   If the developed software contains a structure that obstructs further development, the problem should be restructured whilst retaining the functionality (see Section 2.7). Unit testing guarantees that there are no side effects as a result of refactoring.

Pair programming   In XP projects, developers work in pairs (see Section 2.8) to improve the quality of the software. Knowledge about the software system also spreads quickly as the pairs are changed every now and then.

Collective ownership   In XP projects, all developers are responsible for the whole system (see Section 2.9). In particular, any source code may be changed by any developer at any time. This ensures that individual developers are not indispensable. If a developer is unavailable, any other developer can carry on the work.

Continuous integration   In XP projects, changes are integrated as quickly as possible (see Section 2.10), enabling the whole team to test changes straight away. The overall integration cost is reduced since conflicts are recognised earlier and can be eliminated.

Coding standards   Pair programming and collective ownership can only work if the source code is uniform. In order to do this, pragmatic coding standards are defined (see Section 2.11).

Sustainable pace   In an XP project, the developers should not work overly long hours (see Section 2.12), in order to ensure their creativity and dedication over a more extended period.

Often developers or managers claim that they used XP years ago, maybe with fewer limitations. Kent Beck however says that a project using 80% of the XP practices only achieves 20% of the effects. There is a tremendous difference between a project that uses some of the practices that have been mentioned and an XP project. This does not, of course, hide the fact that very successful projects are carried out without XP. We now outline two project processes: the first uses an extreme opposite of XP while the second uses XP.

1.4 A non-XP project

An existing software system is to be replaced as it is no longer sufficient for the current requirements. To be more specific, the system is not flexible enough and extensions are too expensive. Because of this, the decision has been taken to create a new system with object-oriented technologies. This project is expected to take 12 months.

The project team comprises three developers with experience in object-oriented development and three developers who have training but no experience in object-orientation. In order not to impair the development of existing applications, the developers are only allocated to the project for half of their working time.

In order to have a mature development environment available right from the start, the technology has already been chosen. An integrated development environment, an EJB application server, a Web server with a servlet engine, and a UML case tool are installed on the workstations.

First, a technical analysis is carried out by analysis experts who define requirements, which are described as use cases in the case tool. The processes are described in a textual description and using sequence and activity diagrams. These models are shown to the users so they can be checked and this confirms the correctness of the modelling.

Secondly, the developers tackle the object-oriented modelling of the application system. The system is divided into the technical core concepts, the user interface, and the database connection; each section is modelled by the developers, using the case tool and UML diagrams such as class diagrams, object diagrams, etc. The models are developed in an iterative process in which the developers evaluate their models together and apply the increased knowledge to each model. During the evaluation meetings, a number of technical questions are resolved (performance, failure safety, etc.) and the solutions are also incorporated into the models.

Finally, code skeletons are generated from the diagrams in the case tool and are assigned to the developers for implementation. It soon becomes apparent that the modelled classes cannot be implemented without problems. Some developers devise new classes and others change the relationships between classes or the interfaces of the classes.

The project is not completed on time. After 14 months, pressure is put on the developers and they produce an inconsistent system that contains many errors. Subsequently the development is chaotic. Users find errors in the application and establish that many of their requirements were not implemented adequately. The developers are informed of this and they try to implement the changes as quickly as possible. In this process, the internal structure of the application degenerates and the cost of future changes increases further. In the end, things are no better with the new software than with the old system.

Evaluation of the project

Developers that have just started to learn object-orientation (OO) are initially not as effective as developers with OO project experience. During the planning of the project, therefore, we must take into account the fact that half of the developers are not particularly effective to begin with. These developers will also slow down the experienced developers by asking them questions, etc.

Assigning developers to work part-time on a project is as common as it is ineffective. The change in context between projects means that developers are less productive, thereby increasing costs. Our experience is that developers who are assigned to a project for 50% of the time produce not 50% but only 30–40% of their maximum potential. It is better to have fewer developers working full time on a project.

It is not a particularly good idea to buy technologies before having a rough idea, at least, of what will be developed. The technologies can increase the complexity in the project and it may not be clear to inexperienced developers how they are to be used.

Software development is first of all a learning process. Developers need to understand how users work and what requirements they have for the software. If a technical analyst moves between the user and the developer, a 'Chinese Whispers' game takes place and obstructs the learning process; this can lead to misunderstandings.

It is our experience that users can understand and evaluate UML use cases. It is generally not a good idea to show them sequence or activity diagrams that they cannot really evaluate. Users will approve such diagrams as satisfactory as long as they contain the concepts that are important to them.

The core concepts of the application should not be strictly separated during the modelling phase: they have to be known to and used by the whole project team. Such a division may seem obvious to software developers but, as a rule, it leads to time-consuming modelling. In particular, the modelling of technical components such as the database link are not directly connected to the requirements; when the developers try to cover every conceivable requirement, they produce models that are much too complex. The trend towards complex models is exacerbated by the discussion of technical aspects such as performance and failure safety. As a rule, at this time the developers have hardly any idea about the requirements in this area. And even if these requirements are fairly clear, the developers still do not know how the modelled systems will be put to use. Consequently, the developers increase the complexity of the modelling in order to foresee every possible problem. This leads to unused technologies, which simply means a waste of money.

The allocation of classes to developers leads to a high 'truck factor'.[2] If the assigned developer is unavailable, the training of another developer in the class is very time-consuming. If an assigned developer does not manage to keep a deadline (for example, because of illness), the other developers do not continue to develop his code but work around it. The truck factor is not decreased by modelling all required classes beforehand in a case tool. Our experience is that the models must be changed during programming. When these changes occur, the original models are of little use because they do not reflect the current state of the developed system.

In general, it is bad when analysis, design and construction are separated. These activities should be closely linked because they show up gaps and uncertainties in the technical analysis or the design during the programming.

1.5 An XP project

The same project would run differently as an XP project: the developers are involved in the project full-time; the project team puts its cards on the table with regards to the levels of ability and knowledge of the developers; and it is clear to the experienced developers that they will have to train the less experienced developers.

First, the programmer makes an initial technical analysis in direct communication with the user. All the documents and diagrams are only used for learning and could subsequently be thrown away. Therefore, the developers make their notes on paper or on a blackboard. If a drawing on a blackboard is so important that it should be kept, it is photographed with a digital camera or is drawn with a suitable drawing program.

As soon as the developers have a first overview, they start on the programming. At the beginning, they still have a fuzzy picture of the system that is to be developed. They therefore create programs in order to clarify unanswered questions concerning the system requirements as well as technical aspects. The prototypes are an important tool which can be used by users and developers to form a general understanding of the system that is being developed.

After it is clear which parts of the system have to be developed first, the developers, customers and users create a plan for the first iteration which normally covers a period less than four weeks.[3]

2. The 'truck factor' describes the likelihood of project failure if a specific developer is not available to the project, for example, because the developer is run over by a truck (see Section 2.8).

3. In the field of XP, four weeks is a relatively long time for an iteration and should be seen as an upper limit.

The developers estimate the cost for the individual requirements and the customers and users decide the sequence in which requirements are implemented.

The developers finally produce the planned range of functions – no more and no less. If technical ambiguities appear during the programming, the developers ask the users directly. Several times a day, developers integrate their work into the project repository, enabling a completely functional system to be created at any point in time. It is then no catastrophe if the developers do not produce the entire functionality in the four weeks: at the end of the iteration, they deliver the system as it has been achieved so far. On the basis of this experience, the developers correct their estimating procedure in order to be able to give a more accurate estimation for the next iteration. Even if the developers have estimated incorrectly, the users have received an operational system that contains the most important functions, at the time that was planned. In this way, work continues until all the desired functionality has been produced; new requests can be reacted to flexibly.

Evaluation of the project

The full-time assignment of the developers to the project ensures that the developers can concentrate fully on the project and removes the drop in productivity because of the change between projects. The openness concerning the abilities of the developers is due to the XP principle of open and honest communication and helps to avoid unpleasant surprises later.

The technical analysis is carried out in close contact with the users. Therefore, it has already been accepted in this early stage of the project that the users play an important part in the development of the system. The developers keep in close contact with the user during the whole project because they know that the requirements specification does not decide the success of the project. It is the user that decides on the success or failure of the project. The project is a success only if the user can use the system meaningfully.

The developers stay modest. In particular, they develop only the necessary functionality and not what appears interesting to them. They concentrate on the technical requirements and understand that the technology is a means to an end.

The short iteration cycles make sure that the user always gets accurate and reliable information about the state of the project. The user can be sure what was produced and can be sure of its quality in practice, because of already delivered releases.

In a large XP project, two to three iterations are quite often combined to form a single release.

1.6 Overview of the book

Chapter 2 describes each XP practice in detail. For each practice there is a short description, which focuses primarily on our practical experiences and recommendations.

Chapters 3 to 8 deal with special topics that cannot be associated directly with an XP practice. Chapter 3 discusses the roles that are adopted in the framework of an XP project. Chapter 4 then looks at a number of artefacts that can be used for an XP project. Following this, there is an accurate analysis of how XP projects can be organised and the organisational conditions that have to be fulfilled (see Chapter 5). Chapter 6 is dedicated to the introduction of XP within companies. Our experience of operating in very diverse project environments has taught us that XP has to be implemented and adapted for different contexts. Chapter 7 describes our experiences from the areas of framework development, product development, migration from Legacy systems, e-business, outsourcing, and certification. Throughout the book we refer to experiences that we have gained in various projects; Chapter 8 describes three of these projects in detail.

The text refers to appropriate literature but these references are by no means comprehensive. At the end of each chapter, there is an annotated bibliography that contains additional references.

To conclude, we have set up a Web site where you will find new information, interesting links, and corrections and additions:

http://www.jwam.org/xp-book

1.7 Literature

Agile Alliance. *Agile Manifesto.* http://www.agilealliance.org

Extreme Programming is an agile process. A number of people, other than the fathers of XP, have also done interesting things with the Agile Alliance in order to retain the foundations of flexible, lightweight software development.

Beck, Kent. 2000. *Extreme Programming Explained: Embrace Change.* Reading, Massachusetts, Addison-Wesley.

In this first book on XP, the benchmark for the topic, Kent Beck describes the foundation and general considerations of XP. The book gives a good overview of XP and the philosophy behind it but contains few details. As an introduction, it is an absolute must.

XP practices

In this chapter, we will introduce XP practices. For each practice we will give a short description, explain our experiences, and on this basis give recommendations for how it can be used. We will also look at how each practice relates to the others.

2.1 On-site customer

Description

The software system is commissioned by a customer. XP invites the customer to take an active part in the development process. The on-site customer defines the requirements of the system in 'user stories'. Unlike with other development methods, XP does not need complete or formal specifications of the requirements. User stories are kept on story cards (the 'playing cards' in the planning game, see Section 2.2). They are short, informal stories that describe the features of the system from the perspective of the user.

Availability of the customer

Usually, customers cannot spend 100% of their time working on the project. They can go on with their everyday work but must be available for questions at any time. This means that the developer and the customer should not work in different places.

Example

In an insurance company, an XP project is set up to support the definition of insurance products. The project is equipped with eight developers and one customer. The customer is an employee of the product department which will use the subsequent system. The customer is available for the project 80% of his time. He knows the technical requirements and the business and political interests of his department.

During meetings, the customer gives the developers an initial idea of the requirements of the new system. In this context, things are pared down to a single main system component: the software tool that defines product. The customer writes, on story cards, the appropriate user stories covering the most important aspects of the system from his perspective. Using the resulting 12 story cards, the customer and developers perform the planning game and produce an easily comprehensible set of story cards for the next iteration.

The customer works in the same building, on another floor, and is easily available for discussions and questions. The customer has daily meetings with the developer to obtain a brief progress report (see also Section 5.5 on stand-up meetings). The developers make a new version of the system available to the customer to test every week.

Experiences

Full-time and part-time customers

It is difficult to get a qualified customer dedicated full-time to the project. After all, a good employee is needed by his department at all times. Frequently we have to make do with a 'part-time customer'. In our experience, this does not cause a big problem if there is agreement that developers can talk to the users at any time. In fact, a full-time customer may even lead to problems in long-running projects. In insurance companies and banks, it has been the practice for decades to make a user available full-time to development projects. However, this means that the user becomes more and more removed from the work practice of his colleagues during the course of the project and is increasingly perceived as being in IT. After six months, the user has only a fuzzy idea about how their colleagues in the operational department are working. Developers should be conscious of this problem so they can recognise this danger early on and be able to react appropriately if necessary. This problem can be solved, for example, by substituting customers or through a stronger integration of additional users.

Substitute the customer

Sometimes, the developers do not have access to users due to the project type, for example because a standard product is being developed. In this case, one would have to think how the user can be substituted, perhaps by assigning the role of the customer to someone from the development organisation. It may even be appropriate to bring in additional employees with the necessary subject knowledge. In larger organisations, the product manager can take on this role. Product development is discussed in Chapter 7.

Multi-channel applications

Many of the systems being developed today are 'multi-channel' applications intended to support completely different user groups. For instance, a tariff calculator for insurance products may have the same calculation core but different user groups access it through different front-ends. These user groups may include Internet customers, brokers, sales representatives, office workers and product specialists. It is almost impossible to find a customer that can adequately represent all of these user groups. Any one person will be inclined to show preference to his own user group, not because of maliciousness but because he has insufficient knowledge of the interests and requirements of the other groups.

In such cases, other users can be included as there are several customers in the project, but it leads to additional issues of coordination. Alternatively, a single customer representative can bring the interests of all the customer groups into the project. This is made possible by an additional communication step: the customer representative is responsible for talking to the other customers and for presenting their interests and requirements to the developers.

Customer vs. user
In essence, XP combines the sponsor and user into the role of the customer. This can lead to problems if the user interests and the business interests of the customers are not reconciled. If this happens, neither the 'genuine' customer nor the user can represent both interests adequately. In a similar way to the multi-channel applications, you could introduce a representative who agrees things with the users and sponsor and presents their interests to the developers. However, additional layers in the communication may lead to problems.

Understanding technical implications
Widespread use of data processing has given rise to a disastrous problem: users may have a high level of knowledge in their subject area, but they no longer know how to process the information without system support. They give answers such as 'it is like this because the system has calculated it' and 'I always do that if there is an X in this field'.

Users are inclined to think conservatively about their working environment. As a rule, they do not want a completely new system at all, but just want a few fields to be filled automatically with information that is already somewhere in the system. They may also want more flexibility, without the system being more complicated to use. For many systems, this option does not exist, since old solutions reach the limits of their power. As software developers, it is our daily business to imagine systems that do not yet exist with new uses and functionalities. However, it is hard for the users of our systems to think about anything other than the systems they know.

To overcome this problem, we tend to encourage the developers and users to write the story cards jointly. The developers must not be led by their own interests, but must try to understand the customers. They identify important properties of the future system and note these down on story cards. This scheme has given rise to a lot of sound experiences, especially in situations where the users have been strongly moulded by the existing data processing systems.

Recommendations

- Contact with the users is essential. If you can integrate any of the users into the project team, then do so.

- If, as a development team, you do not exactly know the meaning of a technical term in the user domain and how it is implemented, then do not discuss it further: ask a user (directly, by telephone, by e-mail, or at the next meeting).

- If there are alternatives between which you require a decision, let the customer make the decision.

- Think about the role of the customer in your project. Is one customer enough or do you need several customers? Does a distinction have to be made between sponsor and user? Don't shy away from redefining the role of the customer during the course of the project if it appears to be necessary.

Reference to other XP practices

- *Planning game*: The customer participates in the planning game and writes and prioritises the story cards. If questions about the story cards appear during the development, the on-site customer can answer them immediately. If the plan must be adapted, the on-site customer can participate in the modifications of the plan.

- *Metaphor*: Co-operation with the on-site customer is a great deal easier if the system is discussed on the basis of metaphors. This prevents the developers from presenting the customers with technical details and thus baffling them. Metaphors promote communication and mutual understanding of the product that is to be developed.

- *Testing*: On-site customers write acceptance tests and can test the functionality that is produced. Because of this, developers can quickly get feedback about their work and can recognise errors or mis-understandings early on in the process.

2.2 Planning game

Description

During the planning game, the developers and customers sit together and plan the next release or the next iteration of the software. The requirements are noted on story cards, estimated in terms of cost, and are then prioritised by the customers.

The content of the story cards must be able to be tested. If a card is too large (more than a few days' effort), it has to be split up into several stories. If a card is too small (less than one day), several small stories should be combined.

Experiences

Index cards Noting down requirements on index cards is an excellent way of making them real. If a pair of developers are looking for a new task, they simply take the next card and implement it. This makes sure that several developers do not work on the same task at the same time. If the task is finished, the necessary costs can be noted down on the card with minimum effort. The developers can also write remarks on the cards or can pass them on to another development pair.

We have found that A5 ruled index cards work best (other XP projects work successfully with A6 and, for smaller requirements, A7 size cards). It is also possible to write the requirements on a computer and print them out on A4 paper. The printout can then be folded once and stuck onto the index card. The use of a computer for the planning game would obstruct the whole process. Since the requirements are in card form, the planning game can take place in a meeting room.

It is useful to differentiate between story cards and task cards. On the story cards, we describe the requirements from the perspective of the customers. The story cards can be broken down into task cards, if the story card is relatively large or if it can be broken down into tasks that can be processed in parallel. Technical requirements can also be written on task cards. These technical requirements are irrelevant to the customer and, as a rule, cannot be understood by the customer.

Our experiences with the index cards has given rise to a pattern for the content of the cards. This pattern is, however, very dependent on the project. The index cards outlined here should be taken as an example rather than a template. In general, work with index cards has to be established before it can be formalised. It took us about two years to achieve an initial formalisation.

On every card we write the following pieces of information: title, date, author, type of card (technical requirement, technical refactoring, bug), description of the requirement, acceptance test, estimated cost, actual cost, completion date, and developer. This breakdown of information may make sense for other projects, but our model should not be taken on blindly. In some XP projects, only one keyword is written on the index card, which are then only used as memory aids for the developer. If a project gets by with only one keyword this is wonderful!

Estimation Initially, you may try to estimate the cost of every story in person days. But estimation using abstract measurements, such as jelly babies, has a number of advantages. Developers often estimate costs too low, since they assume an ideal situation where they don't make mistakes, don't hang around in useless meetings, and so on.

At first glance, it may seem a little strange to note down the cost of a requirement in jelly babies. But this helps us to concentrate on the costs of the requirements relative to each other. After we have completed the requirements, we can consider whether the jelly baby (the abstract measurement) estimation is really correct or whether the requirement is easier or more difficult to implement than another. If you calculate the cost initially in the abstract measurement, you can then determine the cost in person days.

We note down the actual costs involved on the index card. The difference between the abstract cost and the concrete cost in hours and days is much more difficult, since developers unconsciously include non-programming times to some extent. Let's assume that someone works on four requirements in one day with a partner. He may note down, respectively, costs of 1 hour, 2 hours, 2 hours and 1 hour for the requirements. This means that he has not programmed for two hours of the day. If, however, he makes a card on the day, he will probably note down '1 PaD[1]' on the card and overlook the fact that he has not programmed for two hours of the day because of breaks he has taken.

Load factor This unproductive time can be expressed as the load factor, or velocity. If one has an estimation based on ideal time it has to be multiplied by the load factor to get the real time. It is hard to believe, but in most companies the load factor is between three and five. It is therefore also clear where the productivity of the developers can start to be increased: unproductive time must be minimised. Although it can be difficult to find out what these unproductive times are in order to eliminate them, the effort is worthwhile. The best teams have a load factor from 1.2 to 2.0. These values cannot be any lower, as they represent necessary breaks and coordination time. In this sense, the remaining non-programming hours are not directly productive, but are beneficial to productivity; for example, design sessions are not pure programming time but can be very beneficial for productivity.

Acceptance of To some extent, the concept of the 'planning game' is met with little *'planning game'* approval by management in development organisations and by customers. If they already are under the impression, for whatever reason, that developers do not work but fool around then the term can reinforce this impression. Therefore, when talking to our customers, we use terms such as 'planning workshop'.

Recommendations

- Reduce the load factor in order to increase the productivity of your developers. Do not however proceed blindly. For example, cutting out

---

1. We measure programming time in pair days (or PaDs), rather than in person days.

design meetings certainly reduces the load factor, but does not improve productivity. The starting points are as follows: cut out unnecessary meetings; minimise the number of participants in meetings; tighten up on necessary meetings (design meetings do not require seats); no meeting lasts much longer than 15 minutes; no meeting requires a table; anyone can leave any meeting at any time without having to justify themselves.

- Allocate developers full-time to the project. Do not burden them with additional tasks.

- Use A5 index cards to make the requirements real.

- Only formalise the index cards as much as necessary. If your developers do not know how to work with the index cards, this problem cannot be solved with formalisation.

- Try to make cost estimations using abstract measurements (such as jelly babies).

- Give the whole thing a different name if the customer feels uneasy about the term 'planning game': simply call it a planning workshop or a planning meeting.

- Differentiate between sponsors and users. The sponser provides the aim of the project and the user is the source of knowledge about the use of the system.

- Make sure that the implementation of a requirement does not last for longer than five pair days (or the equivalent in an abstract measurement of estimation).

Reference to other XP practices

- *Small releases*: We can only 'play' meaningfully with the requirements if they are clear. Only then can we develop sufficient understanding of the individual requirements to make reliable estimates of the time it will take. Small releases are the way to keep the set of requirements clear.

- *On-site customer*: During the planning game, the requirements are merely prioritised. It must already have been made clear to developers and customer what each of the requirements means. This only works if a continuous exchange between customers and users is possible.

- *Testing*: Requirements have to be able to be tested. Only if the acceptance tests are clearly defined can a reliable estimation of the costs of the requirements be indicated.

2.3 Metaphors

Description

Every software system is described using metaphors. These can be very simple figurative presentations of how a system functions, which basic assumptions were made, etc. A metaphor defines to some extent the technical architecture of the system (not only the user interface), because in object-oriented systems the structure between the technical objects can (and should) be like those of the borrowed metaphors.

Kent Beck goes so far as to claim that the practice of using metaphors could replace the task of dealing explicitly with the system architecture. In our opinion, however, metaphors are used when working with architectures and can be as useful in defining the architecture as in communicating about the system.

A metaphor only makes sense if it is shared by all those who are involved in the project. This means that it is vital that only one metaphor or one set of metaphors is chosen.

Example

As an example, let's imagine that we are going to construct a system that supports employees who create invoices. One metaphor could be 'paper and calculator'. In this metaphor, the paper holds the information while the calculator computes the invoice. One consequence of the metaphor would be that it is possible to create inconsistent an invoice if the invoice information is changed but the calculator isn't invoked. This may or may not be desirable; it is important that the behaviour of the system can be assessed and discussed on the basis of the metaphor.

Experiences

Metaphors have great potential and can invaluably enrich the development process. In our experience, it is simpler to guarantee the uniformity of large systems with metaphors than without them. A good metaphor has exactly the required properties for the developers to share a common idea and image of the system.

Metaphors are not always easy to use constructively. If you have chosen a general term for your metaphor (e.g. typewriter), there is the question of which properties of a typewriter should be included in the metaphor. Successful metaphors sometimes detach themselves from their model and develop an independent existence. The wastepaper basket thus stands on the electronic desk and not underneath it. If you use the metaphor of the typewriter for word processing you will, for example, exclude automatically moving to a new page. The easiest solution may be to borrow an existing metaphor. We have had good experiences with the metaphors of the WAM approach.

WAM metaphors

WAM is an acronym for 'Werkzeug, Automat, Material' (that is, 'tool, automaton, material' or the 'tools and materials' metaphor). WAM is a framework that draws on the metaphor of a workstation. We talk to our users about work 'materials' such as forms, master documents, etc. In addition, we explain active system parts as tools or automata ('the contract editor', 'the credit editor' or 'the credit application processor').

In the WAM approach, which has been approved in many professional software projects, the metaphors are arranged in patterns for software architectures. Experience shows that someone who is used to an old application has no common ground for understanding a new system and the metaphors are very important. Even the approach of menu structures and discrete functionality is not suitable for describing flexible software tools.

Metaphors are powerful tools for decision making. If, for example, it is a question of whether two tools can be used on one document at the same time, it can be argued that a component can only be worked on at one workstation by one person, although that person may use both a hammer and a screwdriver at the same time. Two users working separately should not work on the same component at the same time. Intuitively, this contradicts the user's usual contact with physical components, which can be found at only one point in time and in only one place. The remedy for this kind of working situation, in a software system, can be the use of the metaphor 'copy'.

The frequent use of the tools and materials metaphor in our development projects lead to new developers who are familiar with WAM being able to find their way quickly. They normally begin their analyses with the materials and then look at the tools that work on the materials.

This orientation also pays off for the users of the system who find their familiar working objects in electronic form and normally quickly learn how to work with the materials using the newly-created tools. Tools are generally made to be task-oriented and therefore make immediate sense to users, in contrast to pure data input masks.

Recommendations

- Take this section seriously, think about metaphors!

- Choose your metaphors carefully, not every metaphor is equally suitable.

- The WAM metaphors can be used as building blocks. They are not specific to a domain and can be adapted and arranged by you. However, they do not represent a universal solution.

Reference to other XP practices

- *Pair programming, planning game:* Common metaphors make communication easier for these practices. Metaphors allow the components of the future software system, the relationships between the components, and the use model to be discussed on a common level that is sufficiently abstract but can still be implemented.

- *On-site customer:* What applies to communication amongst developers is even more important for communication with users. Metaphors help to explain the concepts behind a system.

- *Simple design:* Whilst metaphors can give instructions about what is to be realised in the system, they can also highlight the components that are necessary.

- *Refactoring:* Existing source code can always be looked at with the question of how well it demonstrates the active metaphor. In this sense, metaphors can also be used in refactoring.

2.4   Small releases

Description

In the framework of XP, the time between releases is reduced drastically; software releases are made accessible to the customer in fractions of the usual time span. Of course, this reduction in time also means that there are fewer changes in each of the small releases. The same work that was otherwise done in years is not now completed in a few weeks. However, releases are planned to produce usable software that progresses in a way that can be recognised by the user. A release is not a snapshot of the development in which some things may not work 'because they are being worked on'. On the contrary, a release is a fully usable system.

At first glance, this aim may not appear to be practical in many projects. For example, if payroll accounting in a company is to be replaced by new software, each small release would support an area in which it could reasonably be used. Concrete examples of this can be found in [Jeffries *et al.* 00, Page 49ff.] as well as below.

The aim of small releases is to collect practical experience of the implemented functions of the software. On the basis of feedback, developers can spot early on in the process whether the objectives of the developers and customers are diverging and whether there are any misunderstandings between them. At this point, developers who work with precise specifications and traditional processes will claim that specifications prevent misunderstandings and errors. Over the last few years, experience has shown that this does not work in practice, since changes keep on occurring during development.

Small releases ensure that the developers are developing software that the customer will use. With this type of knowledge and reassurance, further development can be planned more effectively and possible aberrations can be recognised at an early stage. Small releases contribute considerably to minimising risks during the development of software.

Of course, there is always the question of how long a release cycle should be. This depends greatly on the product that is to be implemented. In the next section, we will look in more detail at where the difficulties lie and what time span can be accepted as reasonable for a release. As a rule of thumb, the first release should take no longer than six months and subsequent releases no longer than three months.

Iterations XP projects further divide release cycles, into iterations. At the end of an iteration, the results are presented to the customer and the next iteration is planned. Although in principle, there is a working version of the software, it is not automatically a release. This subdivision is important because, as a rule, a release carries additional cost (e.g. the costs of creating an installation program, training, carrying out installations). Usually these costs cannot be sustained several times a month. An iteration should last between one and four weeks.

Example

An insurance company is to replace a monolithic host system for contracts management. Since a large quantity of batch programs depend on the host system, small releases do not at first appear to be possible. It looks as though the whole system must be replaced, along with all of its host programs.

It turns out, however, that this is not so. Different user groups work with the existing system: employees, insurance agents and insurance brokers. Each of these groups only uses part of the system. Internal business policy dictates that the support for the brokers is to be improved. The brokers need to calculate and propose insurance contracts, which requires a product database that is available on the host system. Since the products do not change very often, this database can be replicated for the brokers. Therefore, one release cycle develops and delivers a tariff calculator that uses the replicated product database. During the next release, this is supplemented with application forms for insurance policies. These forms must send data regarding contracts to the host. It turns out that the existing transfer programs for insurance agents can be used without being changed.

The support for the insurance brokers acts as a solid base for the other user groups. The calculation of tariffs and the application forms are useful to both employees and insurance agents. The employees, however, require the additional ability to process insurance contracts, which apparently needs direct access to the host database. Instead, the developers decide to duplicate the database. The new application forms are now not only transferred to the host, they are also saved in a parallel database on the application server. At first, the processing of new application forms is carried out in the new system, and the old applications continue to be processed by the host system. The database with the new application forms is synchronised with the host system directly before and after the nightly batch run. This ensures that the new application forms are included in the batch processing. Because of the strict separation between the host system and the new system, the synchronisation is relatively easy: during the day, the new system only processes the new contracts on the host; at night, it only processes the batch programs.

In subsequent releases, a batch program from the host system is programmed for the new system (if the batch program is still necessary) and, for quite a while, functionally identical batch programs run on the host system and on the new system. Any necessary changes to the batch programs are made both on the host and on the new system. In principle, a new release is created after the completion of every batch program.

Evaluation of the example
Although small releases may seem at first to be impossible, with a little ingenuity they would have been possible in every project known to us. It does, however, become clear that additional effort is required in order to achieve small releases (in the example, the program for the synchronisation of the databases was additional to the requirements of the new system). In our view, however, the effort is worthwhile every time, since small releases very quickly make in-depth feedback possible and, therefore, they are very important for minimising risks.

Experiences

The first impression from the developer's point of view is often that small releases mean more stress and tighter deadlines. We have all experienced the relatively stressful time before a release and the idea that one will have to face this stress more often, maybe even once a month, frightens many people. In our experience, the situation is by no means so extreme. Certainly, the day when a release is due may be somewhat more hectic and longer than normal. However, we are talking here about a day, not a week or longer, that is going to be more hectic and stressful.

To keep it manageable, a number of preconditions have to be met. On a technical level, it has to be possible to create a release in a shorter time and without any complications. To do this, we recommend that you use a suitable tool. For our Java-based projects, we use ANT (see [Ant]), which allows a release to be compiled in just a few minutes, after appropriate configuration.

Tools help in creating releases
The tool only simplifies the technical creation of releases; it is not the only precondition for facilitating small releases. The development leading up to a release must be planned appropriately to make sure that the release is on schedule. The customers must be included in this process, in the planning game. They have the final decision over the functionality that should be included in the next release. Team work during the planning game makes sure that deadlines are realistic and feasible (see Section 2.2).

From our projects we have also learnt that greater use of unit tests (see Section 2.5) makes the creation of releases much easier. The more that functionality must be tested manually after a release is issued, the more expensive the creation of the release. If an error appears during a manual test, the procedure for creating the release must be repeated. If the number of these errors can be reduced by unit tests, the team profits significantly from the creation of the release.

In one project, we had extremely small releases, delivering a new release to the customer approximately once a week. During the process, we failed to unit-test a function of the system. During the next release, a problem emerged in the manual tests. We had to eliminate this problem before the release, and debugging was extremely stressful because the creation of the release was held up and we were under time pressure.[2] The experience taught us that extensive unit tests have a particularly positive effect on small releases.

Small releases can also bring pleasant rewards and successes. What developer would not be proud and happy that one of the systems that he or she has developed is being used and makes work easier for the users? And how do they feel if the users say that their system is great and working with it is a pleasure!

Small releases are not easy to achieve
We also learnt in our projects that small releases are not always easy to achieve. In fact, most projects should include a 'learning period' before they start to deliver new releases after short periods of time. If the application domain is complex or new, the developers must first develop an overview of it. During this time, as a rule, we develop prototypes in order to check our understanding. These prototypes are only built for learning and do not claim to be usable in practice. They are therefore a concrete kind of *Spike Solution*, as described in [Jeffries *et al.* 00]. We suggest that this learning stage is kept as short and as compact as possible. Depending on the project, one to three months should be sufficient.

No 'Big Bang'
It is not obvious that small releases can apply in projects that replace large legacy systems. People often attempt to replace legacy systems in one go and smaller steps do not seem to be desirable or feasible. We use small releases in which we encapsulate the legacy system without replacing its functionality. To do this, we implement an object-oriented layer which, for example, allows us to access the legacy system with Java. This layer is implemented in such a way that it offers almost no separate technical functionality. It is merely used to access the legacy system and masks the legacy system during the development of the application. We can gradually extend the functionality (by creating 'capsules') and release the capsules around the legacy system. In the end, the new system is implemented so much that it no longer accesses the underlying legacy system and the legacy system is gradually replaced.

Experience shows that this process leads to success much more quickly and in a less complicated way. In contrast, a 'big bang' replacement of an extensive legacy system always carries with it extreme difficulties and risks. In our projects, we always choose small releases and replace legacy systems in extremely small steps.

---

2. In an XP project, you are not allowed to put off a release, in the narrow sense of the term.

Effects of small releases Now that we have looked at how small releases can be implemented, we want to look further at our experience of the effects of small releases. Early feedback means identification of more and more components that need to be improved. For the next cycle, a decision therefore has to be made about which new properties are to be developed and which properties of the last release are to be improved upon. This makes the planning of a release more difficult as improvements to the last release must also be included in the plan and it results in a change to the form of contract.

Kent Beck has discussed the form of contract in a separate paper (see [Optional Scope Contracts]). The basic argument is that customers of fixed-price projects with a fixed functional scope have no advantage over those whose contract is 'weaker'. Working with functional specifications and legal proceedings regarding clever software development projects shows quite clearly that trying to define 'in legal terms' the functions of software in development is an illusion. Even if you can do it, problems arise immediately if the requirements change during development.

We have drawn the obvious conclusion for our projects that we either reduce the costs or complete only small fixed-price projects (a maximum of 200,000 Euro or US dollars) that are pre-projects for the analysis in which prototypes are produced in order to clarify the requirements. In our projects we have tried to make the customers follow this procedure. It is important that we always behave professionally and produce good software in order to build up mutual trust between customers and software developers, on the basis of which we can negotiate short contracts with flexible wording. Our contracts tend only to be a few pages long and sometimes refer to prototypes that are already available.

The positive consequences this kind of mutual trust can have is shown by one of our projects. We agreed a price but, towards the end of the project, we established that we would exceed the price by approximately 20%. This was our problem because we had estimated the price and signed the contract. We therefore decided to absorb these additional costs. Interestingly, when the customer enquired about whether we could get by on the agreed amount, we put our cards on the table and the customer offered to pay half of the additional costs. This customer relationship surprises a lot of software developers but it can be explained easily. The customer saw that we were doing good work and that they were getting precisely the system that they wanted. Since the customer wanted this situation to continue, the customer actively helped the project to become a success for both parties.

In another project, we carried out a two-month prototype development in order to define the aims and create the concept for the system to be developed. During this time, we presented and discussed the prototype every week or two. The prototype development evolved into product development. The experience of prototype development allowed us to set the space between releases to one week and we were able to carry this out successfully.

Prototyping and small releases

It is worth discussing whether this prototype development really provided releases, as they are understood in XP. This project was creating standard software for a partner to sell to customers. It was not software for an individual and we therefore had no relationship with the users. We got our feedback from our project partner, who determined the direction of the product. In this respect, it is not totally comparable to projects with small releases, as described by Kent Beck (see [Beck 00]). However, we consider these as XP releases. The project partner who receives useful weekly releases is a customer to us. Our customer used the releases in order to produce documentation. In this project, the prototyping was approved because the requirements of the system were completely unclear to the customer at the start of the project. He was simply not in a position to describe the requirements in user stories.

However, the success of this project should not hide the dangers that can occur with prototyping. Users may get the impression that the system is already as good as finished. If the prototype is further developed into the end product, no progress may be visible to the user for a long time. Prototyping also encourages developers to ignore issues that are not important to the prototype and possibly leave technical questions unanswered. Frequently, some issues do not emerge until it is too late, for example, that the database link is not as trivial as was first assumed.

To summarise, prototypes are a secondary solution that you can use if it is necessary (e.g. because of completely unclear requirements). If possible, you should create a genuine release. In any event, the development of a prototype should be limited to a short period of time (e.g. two months).

Prototypes and spike solutions

In XP, pre-projects or 'Spike Solutions' take the place of conventional prototypes. These approaches have a lot in common, but spike solutions focus strongly on the questions that need to be answered. (e.g. 'Can the database link work as was envisaged?') The prototype is often used in a similar way but it extends to describing every possible piece of software, even if unfit for use. A complete discussion of the concept of prototyping would be going too far here. It is important that developers – whether they now call it a prototype or a spike solution – are clear about the questions that they need to answer.

Small releases have proved themselves Overall, small releases have proved themselves to work for our projects. Even if not all projects can achieve one release per week, small releases can normally be implemented. Their contribution to the project should not be underestimated.

Recommendations

- For projects in complex or new application areas, develop a prototype to put the requirements into concrete terms.

- Do not choose release cycles that are too long. Cycles that are longer than three months do not make sense in any project. If the release cycles seem to be too tight, the project planning has to be revised.

- Make sure that a release can be used and that it shows real progress. This is the only way that a release can provide feedback on realistic experiences.

- Support the creation of releases with an appropriate tool that enables releases to be created quickly and without complication.

- Replace large (legacy) systems gradually. Do not accept that 'it does not work in this case'. Our experience shows that it always works.

Reference to other XP practices

- *Continuous integration*: Small releases are easier if there is continuous integration in the project. Since a complete functioning state of the entire system can be found on the integration machine at any point in time, releases can be produced from this state. Integration tests and time-intensive activities, such as a total integration of parts of the system that have been developed separately over months, do not apply.

- *Testing*: Acceptance tests are used to measure and plan the progress of the project for the releases. The parts of the system implemented in a release can be read by acceptance tests. In this context, unit tests play a fairly subordinate role but they are essential in testing the current integration. Unit tests have a positive influence over the small releases, but only in connection with continuous integration.

- *Simple design*: It is far easier to create a good design for a small release. The rapid feedback supplied by small releases enable simple designs to be quickly changed and adapted to the current requirements.

- *Planning game*: Iterations and releases are planned within the framework of the planning game. You work out the properties of the system that are most valuable to the user and that should, therefore, be implemented early. This means that the next release cycle is likely to be short and to include important features.

2.5 Testing

In XP there are essentially two types of tests: unit tests and acceptance (or function) tests. Most other kinds of tests, such as module tests and integration tests, can be seen as special unit tests.

Unit tests: Description

Developers write unit tests to test their own classes. They develop classes and unit tests at the same time. The tests for the operations in a class should be implemented before the operations themselves are implemented. In the XP community, this kind of programming is called *Test-First Programming*. There is therefore a closer relationship between programming and testing. The tests are carried out every couple of minutes.

Unit tests that are developed in this way have a number of positive consequences during the programming of classes:

- The implemented operations are executed and tested straight away, and developers quickly get feedback about whether their classes contain bugs.

- Since it is difficult to test complex classes, designs tend to be simpler. From the start, developers design their classes so that they are easy to test.

- If the test is written for a concept of the class before the related operations are programmed, meaningful operation names are found more easily. This is because the class is considered first from the client perspective and not from the 'ego perspective'.

Unit tests should be used not only during the development process. In particular, unit tests have a central position in refactoring. If existing unit tests can run automatically after every change to the system, it can easily be seen whether the change has produced any negative side effects. Unit tests can also support the correction of errors. If an error is found, the test class will be extended so that it diagnoses the error. The error in the tested class can then be corrected.

All current programming languages have freely available frameworks and test tools for the design and automatic execution of unit tests (see [JUnit], [XPWeb]).

With object-oriented systems it is recommended that you write a test class for every class. The test class should test every typical use of the class. As a consequence, every operation of the class is called at least once.

There are a large number of papers on the Web about Unit Testing, Test-First Programming, and Test-First Design (see [Wiki]).

Unit tests: Experiences

Unit tests lead to a clear improvement in the quality of projects. Bugs are discovered earlier and are located faster. Designs are simpler so that they can be tested better. This increases the confidence of the developers in their code. We have repeatedly observed developers going through the tests again and again without having changed the tested code. We put this down to the developers feeling successful when the test is run successfully.

Developers write tests when they are easy to write and can run automatically. The use of suitable frameworks and tools (e.g. JUnit) has utterly proved itself. Of course, the developers must know how to use these tools in order to be able to use them effectively.

Test classes support the documentation of the system. They show the intended use of the classes that are tested. Test classes also document everything that the developers have tested. This is important, above all, in class libraries and frameworks so that the application developers can check what was tested. If all the cases that are relevant to the application developers are not covered, they can simply extend the existing tests and execute them again to see whether the framework or library works for this case.

If class libraries or frameworks are used in the development of applications, it is difficult to locate errors. It is not always easy to decide whether the cause of the problem is in the framework or the application. Test classes can help in the localisation of errors by the application developers extending the framework tests.

In our opinion, it is important that all developers of the project team write tests. It is important that all accept the procedure of writing the tests first, because it is boring and sometimes more difficult to write tests after the class has been implemented. This may be the reason that, even in our projects, writing tests is still not one of the favourite activities. If an individual stops testing, this quickly has an effect on the others, who lose their motivation because the testing is no longer consistent. In this scenario, our experience shows that the testing eventually stops completely. Consistent testing is definitely one of the most fragile practices; developers justify dropping it on the grounds of time pressure or alleged 'untestability' of certain parts of the program. After a test has come to a standstill, it is very difficult to achieve good test coverage again (the Broken Window Theory[3] applies); it is unclear where tests are available and of what quality they are. If you follow the principle of test-first programming this should not happen, so ensure that test-first programming really is adopted.

Broken Window Theory

According to the Broken Window Theory, dirt and destruction attracts further dirt and destruction. In an experiment in the USA, a car was parked with its bonnet up in the Bronx. Within a few minutes, it had been ransacked. A similar car remained parked up in Palo Alto, California, for a week and was untouched. Then a specific panel of the car was smashed up. This broken panel then lead to further damage to the car and after a short while the other panels were also smashed up, the tyres were stolen, etc.

In New York, graffiti is removed as soon as it is discovered. From this, one can assume that it is easier for graffiti artists to embellish a wall with graffiti if they are not the first.

There exists a lot of material on how to test special technologies and specific parts of the system. You could imagine that it is not easy to write a unit test for a Web application or highly interactive GUI parts of your system but don't be afraid of these cases. There is good material on the Web to help you write unit tests for nearly all situations.

Reusing unit tests

By definition, a class must offer all the methods of its parent class. The methods in subclasses may only be redefined within certain limits. We say that the subclasses must have similar behaviour to the superclass.

---

3. The Broken Window Theory was described in [Wilson and Kelling 82]. The experiment was carried out originally by Philip Zimbardo in 1969. Andrew Hunt and David Thomas first made the connection between the Broken Window Theory and software development (see [Hunt and Thomas 99]).

Consequently, the test case of a superclass should also test its subclasses. Perhaps the tests should also inherit from each other. A test class then inherits from the test class which tests the superclass of the class to be tested. This approach is well suited to simple cases. If the system is larger, some difficulties occur:

- Parallel inheritance hierarchies occur, which experience shows are difficult to maintain.

- In Java, it is sensible to write test classes for interfaces as well. Test classes should then inherit from several other test classes if a class fills several interfaces. In Java, however, this is not possible.

- It is difficult to get an instance of the subclass (the object under test) into the test of the parent class. Perhaps the first approach would be to define a factory method `newTestObject()` in the test of the parent class which returns the object to be tested. However, often several objects must be tested in combination. Objects in subclass tests may have to be parameterized, so that the signature of the `newTestObject()` operation would need to change.

We therefore show the inheritance hierarchy between the operational interfaces and classes through the delegation between the test classes. Each test class uses the test classes of the interface and superclasses from which the classes it tests inherit.[4] Each test class creates objects of the class to be tested in the `setUp` method. Also, every test class defines a constructor to which the classes that are to be tested can be transferred.

If, for example, we have derived a `Customer` class from the `Person` class, the `Customer_Test` test class uses the `Person_Test` test class. The `Customer_Test` test class creates a customer object and then calls the `Person_Test` test class with this customer object. If the test was successful, it calls its own test operations with the customer object.

Unit tests as a laboratory for inheriting classes

A big problem with the use of frameworks is the 'semantic shift' in the formation of subclasses. This effect occurs if application developers form subclasses from framework classes and do not stick to the 'rules' for the

---

4. In the spirit of simple design, we start with the simple solution (test classes inherit from each other) and then only use the other variants if we cannot get any further with the first solution.

formation of subclasses. These rules specify the way in which subclasses must be formed so that they can cooperate with other framework classes without any problems. If these rules are not adhered to, anomalies that cannot be located easily occur during the use of the framework.

The problem is that there is no established formalism which can specify how subclasses are formed. This specification is best given as a comment to the framework class. However, this leads to incomplete information and misunderstandings.

Tests for framework classes can put things right here. If these tests are developed so that they can be reused, the application developers can have their classes tested by these framework tests and thus make sure that they have not broken the rules for the formation of subclasses.

Testing and Design by Contract

It is argued that test classes make the 'Design by Contract principle' redundant (see [Meyer 97], [Hunt and Thomas 99]). Others argue the opposite – that test classes are not necessary if Design by Contract is used. Our experience shows that Design by Contract and unit tests supplement each other very well.

Design by Contract is based on the concept of the abstract data types (ADT). As well as the signatures of operations, ADTs specify preconditions and axioms. The preconditions of ADTs correspond directly to those of the contract. The axioms, on the other hand, can only express themselves through the preconditions and postconditions of the contract. The axioms can be implemented as a unit test.

The contract of a class generally specifies for which behaviour the test is to be written. The values with which the parameters must be tested are especially clear, because contracts indicate the range within which valid values lie. The test itself makes sure that all operations are called and that all contracts are checked once.

In practice, contract tests often remain active when the application is being used. Thus, errors that only appear with the user are noted down and can be eliminated later on. This cannot be achieved with unit tests alone.

Sometimes it is suggested that preconditions must also be 'negatively tested'. Negative tests deliberately breach the precondition of an operation and intercept the violation of the contract. The test is only successful if the precondition is also violated. These negative tests are nonsensical for a number of reasons:

• According to the contract, the weakening of preconditions and the strengthening of postconditions in subclasses is allowed. At the same time, we would also like to use the test class of a class for its subclasses.

If the preconditions of the subclasses are weakened, they no longer satisfy the tests of the superior class.

- The contract of a class specifies which cases are dealt with in the model of the class and what lies outside this model. To do this, the contract defines the limits between the defined and still undefined behaviour of the class. If we were to write negative tests for preconditions, we would be claiming that this undefined behaviour is actually defined (as exceptions in the violation of the precondition).

- A negative test of preconditions can have two results: the precondition is violated and the test is successful; or the precondition is not violated, which is regarded as an error by the negative test. However, if all subsequent operations provide correct results despite this, we can hardly call it an error. If the subsequent operations give faulty results, this is uncovered by the tests that follow anyway.

- By definition, contracts may not change the execution of programs (with the exception of runtime). A program in which the contracts are tested behaves in just the same way as the same program in which the contracts are not tested. If you deactivate the testing of the preconditions, the test cases would fail.

Acceptance tests: Description

Acceptance tests (also known as function tests) enable the customer to accept the system. Therefore acceptance tests are also often described as a small 'specification' of the system to be created. Acceptance tests are implemented by tests written from the user's perspective. If the acceptance tests can run automatically, this makes the development a great deal easier.

You might imagine an acceptance test implemented to compare calculated results of the program under test with predefined results in a spreadsheet written by the customer. This is in some way the ideal case: the customer defines the acceptance test and the developer implements the acceptance test to refer in an automated way to the values defined by the customer.

But this is not always the case. We often build interactive systems with a reactive user interface. In such a case, acceptance tests cannot be completely automated because the acceptance criteria do not consist only of calculatable data but also visual behaviour on screen. The latter is hard to test automatically with justifiable expense. Therefore, as a rule, the automated acceptance tests only cover the functional portion. A manual acceptance test carried out by the customer is also necessary in many cases.

Manual acceptance tests do, however, carry the danger that the description of the acceptance test is interpreted by the tester and uncertainty arises. The acceptance test then offers restricted security for developers. They can no longer be absolutely sure about whether the customer requirement has been implemented. Also, manual acceptance tests quickly become impractical in large systems.

Since acceptance tests specify the requirements of the system, they can be used to control progress in the development project. This does not exactly mean that the system is 50% ready if half of the acceptance tests are running. However, the number of acceptance tests that are fulfilled is a true indication of the progress of the project, whilst stagnation or even a reduction in the successful acceptance tests points to problems in the development process. Acceptance tests are a powerful instrument for the management of projects.

Acceptance tests: Experiences

Acceptance tests as a component of the contract

Our experiences indicate that acceptance tests are suitable for communicating with the customer as well as for controlling progress in the project. If acceptance tests are included in the contract between developers and customers, it can lead to problems in the development process. Acceptance tests that are, for example, a component of a fixed-price contract, have additional – legal – requirements. Sometimes this leads to a tough fight between the legal representatives of customers and contractors. If this is the case, the writing of the acceptance test takes an excessively long time and it is better to distinguish between the contract and the acceptance tests.

GUI capture/ playback tools

In principle, acceptance tests for visual applications with an interactive user interface can be recorded and executed with GUI capture/playback tools. Experience with these tools shows, however, that their support for cyclic development processes is still weak. The cost of changing tests is too high.

Dummy classes for the GUI library

As an alternative, one of the tools for unit tests can be extended. With the help of dummy classes, acceptance tests can be programmed in the same way as unit tests. However, the way the tests are used is different. Whilst unit tests always have to achieve 100% success, this requirement is not valid for acceptance tests. We can write acceptance tests using a widely-used framework for unit tests. In the simple case, the test tool may carry out unit tests and acceptance tests separately from one another and report the results separately.

Persistent data can cause problems when formulating automated acceptance tests, in particular if large databases from a legacy system need to be integrated into the development. In such cases, the provision of a meaningful and explicit database can be a full time task for several developers.

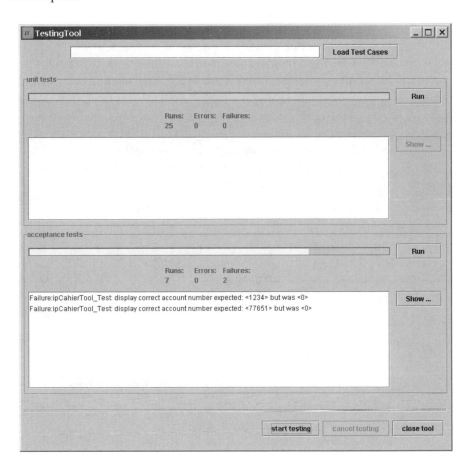

Figure 2.1 Extended tool for unit and acceptance tests

Who writes acceptance tests? An important question is who writes the acceptance tests. Since they define in practice the perspective of the customers on the system, it is natural to have the acceptance tests written by the customer.

However, we must match this ideal situation to the abilities of the customers. If the acceptance tests are programmed in a similar way to unit tests, this can of course only be done by the developers. Writing good acceptance tests is a skill to be learnt: acceptance tests must be as accurate as possible and must also be able to be tested. Therefore, it is sensible if the developers are provided at least some support in the writing of acceptance tests. We have carried out projects, which were mainly about micro-economic calculations, in which the customer wrote the acceptance tests (which are predominantly expressed through formulae) themselves, without any support from developers.

To control the progress of the project, we tried to combine the checking of unit and acceptance tests within one tool. Therefore we extended a JUnit-like testing framework to check and display unit and acceptance tests on one screen (see Figure 2.1). The tool shows the unit tests at the top via a general JUnit interface. Below, the acceptance tests are executed via a similar interface. The only difference is that failed acceptance tests cause the bar to become yellow instead of red. You may also imagine dividing the acceptance testing bar into a green part (showing the completely implemented acceptance tests) and a yellow part (showing the acceptance tests that do not run yet).

Recommendations

- Write a test class for every class (GUI or JSP-generated classes could be an exception) and call every operation of the class to be tested. If a single test class becomes too complex, several test classes can be created for a class.

- Group the tests inside one test class by concepts, not by methods. A test class that contains the same methods (prefixed by 'test') as the class under test gives a bad smell: the design is based on methods rather than concepts.

- Use one of the test tools for unit tests (e.g. [JUnit], see also [XPWeb]) and extend it to your special needs. The test tools have a number of additions available.

- Let all the tests run consistently and frequently.

- Prevent classes from being integrated into the project repository until all unit tests are green.

- Proceed in a test-driven way.

- Use unit tests and Design by Contract for all your classes.

- Do not implement any negative tests for pre and post conditions.

- Carry out a refactoring for tests if this appears to be reasonable. Test classes must also be easy to understand.

- Ensure that all team members write tests.

- Use acceptance tests to control progress of the project.

Reference to other XP practices

- *On-site customer*: Testing on different levels plays an important part in the integration of customers. If we have a good coverage of the system with unit tests, the user is not hindered by simple bugs during the testing of the acceptance criteria. The wishes of the customers are directly connected with the acceptance tests so that the developers can check the acceptance criteria before they give the software to customers to test.

- *Simple design:* A simple design is easier to test than a complex one. Simple design is promoted by means of the convention of writing a test class for every class.

- *Planning game:* The acceptance tests are very important in the planning game. They specify the extent of a story card: for every story card, the developers can test whether they were fulfilled. Developers can be certain about which story cards they have implemented in accordance with the customer requirements, in an iteration. As well as this, they can also be used to control progress in the project. The number of confirmed acceptance tests clearly says a lot more to the developers and customers about the progress of the project than statements such as '80% of the classes are coded'.

- *Small releases*: Before a release the software needs to be tested. In the process, it has to be guaranteed that all functions that were possible with the previous release are also possible with the new version. With small releases, this requirement is only met at realistic cost if automated unit tests are available and the acceptance tests are formulated clearly.

- *Continuous integration*: Continuous integration is only possible if the unit tests achieve good coverage. Otherwise, there is great danger that an operational system is 'damaged' by an integration.

- *Collective ownership*: Collective ownership profits considerably from unit tests. The unit tests define the requirements that classes must meet and guarantee that, if a change is made, a requirement is not inadvertently 'destroyed'.

- *Pair programming*: We always program in pairs and this also applies to the writing of test cases. The partner must make sure that test cases are written during the development of a class.

- *Refactoring*: Refactoring is only possible if there are enough unit tests available. Otherwise, the danger of producing undesirable side effects through refactoring is too great. Unit tests are also subject to refactoring if they can be structured better. Unit tests are not second class source tests!

2.6 Simple design

Description

Good design is indispensable for software. This is no different for XP projects. There is always the question of what a good design is and how many designs should be created for what and when.

A trained extreme programmer answers this question with a counter-question: what is the simplest thing that could possibly work? XP software development uses a lightweight process and can react quickly and easily to changes. Therefore, with XP, there is no 'big upfront design' to follow; design is confined to the most necessary parts. This does not mean that without any kind of design you can just 'program away', quite the opposite. Design is important for software development; it is also seen as important in XP projects, where design continues throughout the development process. This means that the developers can create an optimal design for a problem at any time. If the conditions that created a design change, the design can be revised and the current circumstances can be accommodated by a more appropriate design.

In order to make this possible, we must look at design in a different way. The designs that are created in an XP process are not all-inclusive and do not represent a complete system. They always refer to a small section of a specific problem which is easy to understand and must be solved at this point in time in the process. These designs solve a small problem well and can be implemented quickly. If a design is produced at an early stage, it can be tested very early on in the development. Bad design decisions can be discovered quickly and changed easily. What is good design today can be bad design tomorrow. The secret of small designs is that they can be changed more easily than large, heavy-duty designs.

Simple design must be pursued consistently in an XP process. As a rule, for a good design, Kent Beck says that no logic should be implemented twice (the 'Once and Only Once' principle, see Section 1.3). If a piece of logic is implemented a second time, in a new or changed part of the system, the design should be revised (an appropriate refactoring is necessary, see Section 2.7). Kent Beck provides four guidelines that characterise simple design (see [Beck 00], Page 109) in a system (the source code and the test classes):

- The system should express everything in a comprehensible way.

- The system should contain no duplicated code.

- The system should contain as few classes as possible.

- The system should contain as few methods as possible.

These guidelines should be used additively: the sequence of the list implies prioritisation of the points. For example, a reduction in the number of classes and methods should not be at the expense of making the system less comprehensible.

One the one hand, simple design helps the creation of easily comprehensible designs that progress faster and more clearly. This makes it easier to handle and change the total system. On the other hand, simple design prevents us from building up a stock of technology. You may often hear a developer say something like 'OK, this is not important for this story card now, but we will need it soon anyway'. Do be careful: this kind of supply inventory hogs resources at the wrong time. Under the premise that the feature will have to be implemented, it may seem not to matter when it is implemented. This is very wrong! It makes a big difference.

A stock of technology is, by definition, not needed at the time of its implementation. Consequently, the feature will not be activated when the system is used and it is not included in practical tests. This means that the feature is not given a lot of attention during the refactoring and the relevant classes only satisfy the degenerated pseudo-tests or the tests are confined to ensuring that the class can be compiled. Furthermore, the feature may often be implemented more easily and more elegantly at a later stage.

If you delay the implementation for as long as possible, the feature will probably cost less. This is, of course, only true if the design and the implementation of the application will be improved permanently and systematically. If you put off the refactoring and other improvements for too long, the development will inevitably be slower and more sluggish, and then new features or changes will also become laborious and time-consuming.

Apart from the fact that features not yet required will, in all probability, be implemented more easily and better at a later stage, another problem with the supply inventory is that the developers often cannot know for certain whether the property will be needed in the future. If it is not required, and this happens every day, the development organisation has incurred needless expense.

A stock of technology can be compared with a company's physical resource planning. In both cases, one tries to store goods for as short a time as possible, since storage costs money and does not make any profit. Minimal storage costs arise if the goods are sold directly after production. It is precisely this optimisation that is one of the aims of XP.

If a project has to deal with changes in the preconditions, requirements, or other conditions, and this situation arises frequently in most projects, a simple design can react more quickly.

Quick Design Sessions Even during the creation of a design, the emphasis is on gaining feedback as quickly and easily as possible. This is the only way that you can be completely sure that you have created a good design. XP projects carry out a 'Quick Design Session' in which a few developers sketch out a design on a white-board and discuss it. This should be as brief as possible and should not lead to endless discussions. It is best to try out a design by implementing it and then create a new or modified design if there are any difficulties.

Kent Beck recommends that you should not 'make two design decisions in a row'. As soon as the first design decision has been made, you should implement it and then discuss things further on the basis of the knowledge that has now been acquired.

Test-first design An important practice is 'test-first design', in which the test class is written before the class to be tested. Experience shows that this encourages simple design.

Experiences

Small, simple designs are easy and quick to change. This property evades us if the basic conditions or the requirements of the system are changed frequently. There is still the fear that, if too few designs are made in advance, changes to the system are more difficult to implement because they were not thought through beforehand. People are often convinced that planning certain properties of the system beforehand will save expense later on and so the complete system will not be affected in a negative way later.

This concern is justified. If the XP team does not have enough experience with similar systems and if it puts off for too long a necessary refactoring and changes to the design, later changes may prove damaging to the project. In our projects, we therefore arrive very early on at some idea of the macro architecture of the system that is to be developed.

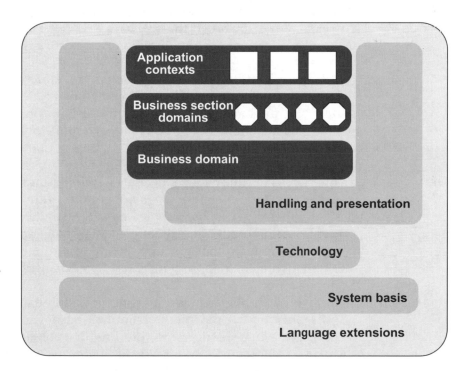

Figure 2.2 An example layer architecture from [Züllighoven]

The macro architecture (see [Züllighoven 02]) determines the general structure of the system to be developed. It should therefore identify basic components of the system and explain the relationships between them.

The layer model (see Figure 2.2) is an example of this kind of macro architecture, based on [Bäumer *et al.* 97].

This architecture identifies layers that help us to structure the system to be developed. The content of the layers and the relationships between them are clearly described. Thus the developers know, for example, that an 'account' document will definitely not be found in the system basis layer, but in the business domain.

Metaphors, used in the same way as in XP projects, supplement the presentation of a macro architecture with finer layers and help the developers to look at the system from a common point of view. But we do not only use metaphors among the developers. Metaphors are also an elementary way to get regular feedback from the users.

Using a suitable macro architecture and appropriate metaphors, it is possible for us to make the structure of the software similar to the application domain. This means that the structure of the application domain immediately results in our software and there is a high correspondence between the software and the application domain. Concepts and terms of the application domain can easily be found in the software.

For example, this perspective of the system, enriched by appropriate design patterns, forms a rough architecture for an interactive workstation system. On the basis of this, an architecture that has already proved sustainable in a number of projects is used. On the one hand, the project benefits from objective experiences and, on the other, the architectural perspective prevents you from going in the wrong direction. And the macro architecture is flexible enough to let the developers move flexibly.

An architecture, therefore, does not conflict with the idea of simple design in the XP sense, but supplements it. A suitable architecture also prevents you from not noticing fundamental changes until later. This, of course, presupposes that the architecture was suitably chosen for the application domain. If this is not the case, later changes to the architecture become a lot more difficult.

In XP projects, the architectural concept traditionally does not have a good reputation: it represents complicated design and 'a stock of technology'. When we suggest, despite this, that you have a rough idea of the macro architecture, it seems a bit like tightrope walking. On the other hand, if you have no idea of the architecture, it almost borders on ignorance. In general, developers have an idea of an architecture at the back of their minds. If the unspoken architectural ideas in the team clash, this can lead to unpleasant difficulties.

One therefore has to bear in mind the architectural perception with regards to the J2EE specification: JSP pages display information, servlets process them and communicate with Session Beans. These in turn use Entity Beans, with which the data management is regulated. This is a definitive architecture, in contrast to the simple set of technologies promoted within the J2EE.[5]

Architecture and responsibility

Traditionally, architectures are used to allocate responsibility. Thus each developer is given responsibility for one or more system components. This is definitely no longer an XP approach. Instead of using the architecture to divide responsibilities within one team, we try to use the architecture to organise the collaboration of several XP teams. Several XP teams initially develop in an organic way: if they become too large, they split into two teams. When they split, it must be clear how the two new teams are to work with each other. There is little experience of how this works in practice. An architectural perception could be helpful in defining the two new teams. It is possible that the architecture grows in parallel with the division of the team.

Architectures, for the moment, are no reason to program some kind of infrastructure. Even if, for example, fundamental layers of technology in the layer architecture are shown, they are not defined or even constructed at the beginning. They arise during the implementation of technical requirements. It is seldom a good idea to divide teams horizontally with the architecture. If this were done, there would be a team responsible for the technical requirements and one for the infrastructure. As a rule, this leads to the second team working at a distance from the concrete technical requirements and it is likely to produce 'a stock of technology'.

Flexible handling of macro

A rigid macro architecture would prevent flexible work on simple solutions. We therefore use macro architectures flexibly and adapt them to our current needs. Refactoring and simple designs are thereby possible. In addition, a loose coupling between the components is promoted by the architecture and a loosely-coupled system is much easier to refactor than a highly-coupled one.

What is a simple design?

Architecture and simple design therefore do not contradict but supplement each other in a meaningful way. There is still the question of what a simple design is or when a design can be regarded as being simple.

As a rule, nothing more than a qualified developer and a whiteboard are required to create a good, simple design. At first this sounds like a stereotype, but it gives us a good clue as to the extent of a simple design. If the design takes up more than one or two whiteboards, it is too large. A simple design can be created well in a 'Quick Design Session' and can be implemented without excessive cost.

---

5. The technologies used in the J2EE environment (e.g. Application Server) are not an architecture, however. A number of different architectures can be implemented using these technologies.

Documentation of designs   In our experience, large CASE tools have not proved very useful for the documentation of simple designs. An application for drawing diagrams (such as, Visio from Microsoft) is normally sufficient. Digital cameras are also useful for putting the image on the whiteboard quickly and easily onto paper.

In our projects, simple designs have been a great help and we transfer this idea to other areas of the development process. We try to keep the code as clear and simple as possible and not to implement any constructs that are too complicated. Even the process itself can be kept as clear and simple as possible, so that we can adapt it to changing requirements in a flexible way and are not constrained within a rigid structure.

In our opinion, simple designs are particularly suitable for projects in which the requirements are unclear or often change and in which we have to react flexibly. Under such conditions, the aim of the project can be achieved much more smoothly following the principle of simple design.

Establishing simple designs

Establishing and introducing simple designs is not an easy task. A big problem with simple designs is that they do the exact opposite of what many computer scientists have learnt over many years and which is still common today: finding common solutions, developing with a view to the future, anticipating requirements and changes, and much more.

In projects, simple designs create a high potential for conflict, since different opinions clash with each other and the developers in the initial phase of their XP activity find it difficult to get accustomed to these new ideas. At this point, it is important to use an XP coach (see Section 3.5) and to insist on simple designs that can be easily and quickly implemented.

Simple design and frameworks

A principle for simple design is that technology should not be built up front. The developers should develop a simple design for the current problem and not think about possible future requirements and designs. This seems plausible for product development and can be directly implemented. For the development of frameworks, this approach at first seems contradictory. A framework can be regarded as a pure stock of software (or design). In frameworks, we show general solutions and abstractions, which will be used to remedy a number of similar problems.

Whilst we have been developing the JWAM framework (see [JWAM]) over the last three years using XP practices, we have asked how we were going to use the XP practice of simple design. Certainly the basic way of tackling things in the development of frameworks is driven by experience and stimulation from application development. As a rule, frameworks are not developed in a void, but on the basis of experience that has been gained and the analysis of several applications of a similar nature. Simple design can transfer very well to frameworks because the framework should only be equipped with as much design as is necessary to solve the problem, no more. In the process, the 'problem' here marks a part of the application that could be implemented with a framework which, for example, could be reused in order to make the application simpler.

Thus the basic principle of a simple design for frameworks is clear: only integrate elements into the framework with which several existing applications become simpler to refactor. This can be reduced to the simple phrase: use before reuse.

In cases in which we have no access to the actual applications, we formulate the requirements with story cards and use examples. This happens if the wishes and suggestions of the JWAM customers suggest how the framework should be developed further. Thus we protect ourselves from keeping too many framework features in stock.

Optimising performance

Discussions about simple designs frequently lead to a heated debate about performance optimisation. When should one think about the performance of the system? When should performance be optimised? Is it not inevitable, if we use simple designs, that at the end of the development there will be a complex system that has serious problems with performance?

First of all, we stick by the idea that such ill-conceived systems should not occur in a good XP development process since the design of the system is always suited to the current requirements. Refactoring makes sure that parts of the system that have been joined together are still an adequate implementation of the solution. If performance problems occur during the course of the development, it is simply because it is a non-optimal design for the system which has to be converted into a better design. This does of course presuppose that the other XP practices such as, for example, refactoring, are implemented and that simple designs are continually improved. Creating and modifying simple designs does not mean that you should just forgo design.

As a rule, simple designs perform better than complicated designs since they involve fewer objects and interactions between objects. We follow the guidelines of Butler Lampson and Kent Beck: 'Make it run, make it right, make it fast'. Therefore, we do not start to optimize the performance of the system until the main part of it (or the whole system) functionally satisfies our customer. To optimize the performance we use the appropriate profiler tools to determine the points of the system that are causing poor performance and optimise these specifically. A design that follows the 'once and only once' principle helps in doing this.

In one project, the customer initially put much value on completing the technical functionality. Therefore we focused our whole development capacity on this goal. At the end of the project, the performance of the system needed to be considerably improved. Therefore we specifically identified and weeded out the weak points with a profiler. Because we continually improved the design during the development, we were in a position to implement the optimisations with as little effort as possible.

Overall, XP is the development process of choice for constructing systems that can be easily profiled and optimised.

Recommendations

- In a design session, do not create any design that does not fit on one or two whiteboards.

- Strive to move quickly from design to implementation. No design session should last longer than half a day.

- Limit the number of participants in a design session to a maximum of five. Three people is an optimal number. More participants than this may have a negative effect.

- Practice test-first design.

- Do not leave bad designs unchanged for too long. Change them as quickly as possible (see Section 2.7).

- Only optimise performance if you have a performance problem. Profiling tools can help to find weak points that can be specifically eliminated.

Reference to other XP practices

- *Refactoring*: The concept of simple design provides a guideline for refactoring. Refactoring is only sensible if it simplifies the design. In the same way, simple designs make sure that existing code can be changed quickly and easily, for which a refactoring is preferable.

- *Testing*: Simple designs and simple classes are easier to test than complex ones. A simple design benefits from testing. This leads to classes being formed as simply as possible so that they can be tested more easily.[6]

- *Small releases*: Small releases provide quick feedback as to whether the system being implemented lives up to expectations and whether it is developing in the right direction. We can therefore quickly see whether the design of the last release is wrong and needs to be changed. By means of simple designs we make sure that we only create designs that are actually needed for the release. This reduces the risk of changes in the design.

- *Pair programming*: Simple design is promoted by pair programming. Regular reviews lead to the implemented design being simple and easy to understand and the partner at the computer makes sure that the design is not bad or unsuitable.

- *Metaphor*: Metaphors determine the general direction of the development of the system and therefore ensure that the simple designs are on target. The frames in which the simple designs can move are set through the metaphor or metaphors used.

- *Sustainable pace*: One of the aims of simple design is that the changes can be implemented quickly and easily. Simple design and modularised refactoring means that changes can be implemented in small steps and in a shorter time. Consequently, the danger of having to work overtime to get the system running again is reduced considerably. Simple designs thus contribute the developer being able to go home with a clear conscience after a 40-hour week.

2.7 Refactoring

Description

Software development practice contains the guideline 'Never change a running system'. This guideline arises from experiencing undesirable side

---

6. However, for the testability of a class, it may also be the case that the interface of the class must be extended with special operations. This can be necessary if objects used by the class have to be replaced by mock objects (see [Mackinnon *et al.* 2000]).

effects due to changing a running system. All too often, a change to a software system leads to undesirable side effects at a completely different point in the system. Therefore, changes to the system are limited to those that are absolutely necessary. In particular, changes that only improve the internal structure are not carried out. This leads to the well-known signs of aging software: 'historically grown' structures arise, maintenance of the system becomes so time-consuming that there are no more resources available for redevelopment, and finally the system becomes unmaintainable.

Refactoring in XP is the restructuring of a software system whilst retaining its observable behaviour. The aim is to improve the design in order to keep the cost to a minimum. By means of refactoring, the structure of a software system can be made flexible and can be regularly adapted to the current requirements. With refactoring, we enhance the system with new functionality and improve the existing design without changing the behaviour of the piece of software.

But the idea of refactoring alone is not enough. Refactoring means improving the existing design, which means changing the software. Changes always run the risk of introducing new defects into the software. If the risk of new defects is too high, we won't change the software but that is not the solution. The software has to be changed to remain flexible and changeable. We need a mechanism to allow safe and smooth refactoring all the time.

The regression test facility of the unit tests give us a mechanism that allows us to check the restructured, refactored system. The idea behind this important combination of refactoring and unit testing is: we refactor the program and the unit tests tell us whether we have introduced defects or not. Using this approach, unit tests are a necessary precondition of refactoring. Together, these practices are powerful.

One of the key ideas behind refactoring is also the approach of refactoring in small steps. This allows you to keep a system running, which reduces the risk of doing too much at the same time. Martin Fowler describes the mechanics of refactoring in such a way that every refactoring can be done in small steps (see [Fowler 99]).

The idea of small steps also means that a larger restructuring should be broken down into the smallest possible refactorings. Every refactoring should be able to be executed in just a few minutes, to minimise the danger of errors being introduced and of the development running into a dead end.

Experiences

Psychology

Software developers frequently doubt that every change to a software system can be broken down into small refactorings. Over the last few years, we have made thousands of large changes to software systems. Whilst we were still learning XP, we did not break down every change into small refactorings. And it is precisely these big changes that caused us the biggest problems: undesirable side effects appeared; the changes were extremely time-consuming; branches of code appeared that were difficult to integrate again. We have learnt that every change can be divided up into small refactorings. The ideal size varies from 30 minutes down to 2 to 5 minutes.

The division of a refactoring into small steps is, however, not an easy task. In [Fowler 99], Martin Fowler has described the most common refactorings and how they are broken down. When reading the book for the first time, you may think that there is nothing really new in it. However, when you do some refactoring, you will probably have some problems breaking down changes into smaller pieces. If you then read the corresponding points in the book, you will find that there are a lot of valuable hints and tips in it after all. [Fowler 99] is supplemented by the work of Joshua Kerievsky on refactoring to patterns (see [Kerievsky 02]). He describes a number of refactorings to introduce or remove typical and often used design patterns.

Source code management

If developers carry out fine-grained refactoring, they can integrate the modified source code quickly into the project repository. This enables them to use the version control system with optimistic locking mechanisms. Any developer can change any file at any time. When a developer tries to integrate modified source code into the common repository, the version control system checks whether the file has been modified by another developer in the meantime. If this kind of 'conflict' occurs, the developer cannot integrate the file and has to resolve the conflict. But when refactorings are kept small, the danger of this kind of conflict is low.

Many conventional version control systems implement a pessimistic locking strategy. Developers can only change files that they have locked beforehand. A developer cannot modify a file that is already locked by another developer.

On the one hand, pessimistic locking prevents the conflicts discussed above. On the other hand, developers have to know exactly which files they want to modify in advance. If it then turns out that further files have to be modified, they must be locked more or less laboriously, one by one. In the worst case, the files that are required may already be locked by other developers and the developer has to wait for a colleague to finish his task.

Our experience has shown that pessimistic locking mechanisms inhibit the flow of development and are opposed to collective ownership. Optimistic locking processes work a lot better with an agile development process like XP. They also favour the breakdown of large changes into small refactorings since frequent conflicts caused by integration are effectively prevented.

Goal-oriented *refactoring* Initially, developers may fall into the trap of seeing refactoring as an end in itself. They improve the internal structure over and over again and thus neglect the requirements of users and customers. If this happens, refactoring is not directly profitable for the customers or users who, as a rule, are only interested in the behaviour of the system that can be observed from the outside. The following advice can be used to steer refactorings: only do refactoring that allows the next user requirement to be implemented more easily. Refactoring that is not associated directly with the requirements of the user is superfluous. (We understand bug fixes as a requirement in this context.) On the other hand, refactorings should not be constantly put off in order to implement user requirements (see *Broken Window Theory* on Page 35). This quickly leads to the wishes of the user becoming difficult and expensive to meet.

Frequently, the principle of simple design is referred to in order to justify refactorings. If an implemented design is identified as not being simple enough, refactoring can be carried out. There is however the question of knowing when a design is actually simple enough.

The factors that are described can help to carry out the right amount of refactorings. They do, however, contain a certain amount of leeway. Finding the right balance is not always easy. The longer you experiment with refactoring, the easier it is to make the decision about the correct time for refactoring.

Testing and refactoring

As we already mentioned, refactoring cannot be used effectively without unit tests. Test classes work as safeguards during a refactoring. They make us confident of not introducing new defects while changing the system. If we refactor (and therefore change) a class or a number of classes without changing the test classes and they still run at the end of the refactoring, it must really preserve the behaviour of the class.

The unit tests only safeguard us if they are not changed during the refactoring. Otherwise we may introduce defects into the test cases themselves.

But the requirement not to change the unit tests during refactoring is not self-evident. Consider a simple 'Rename Method' refactoring where we change the name of a method which is a member of the public interface of the class. It is highly probable that the test class uses this method (otherwise the class, especially the method, has not been developed by test-first programming). You have to change the method name inside the test class, too. This example seems not to be complicated or risky because many of the refactoring tools automate this task and ensure the correct preservation of behaviour. You may think of other examples (for example, Split Class) where you also have to change the test class. These examples make the general conflict more obvious.

A possible solution to this dilemma could be to use the same practices and principles for refactoring that we use for normal programming: write the tests first. In refactoring, this principle means that we first change the test class. The developer modifies the test class to test the refactored class, before changing the class under test. Then, of course, the tests fail and we proceed in exactly the same way as we do for test-first programming: we change just enough to fulfil the tests; that is, we implement the refactoring. Frank Westphal calls this 'Test-First Refactoring'.

Refactoring support

The idea of refactoring is also supported by some nice tools. For some time, Smalltalk has had a refactoring browser (see [Smalltalk Refactoring Browser]) that supports the developer with a number of different refactorings. For example, if a developer wants to rename an operation, the refactoring browser renames not only the operation in the class but also changes all uses of the operation to the new operation name. For Java, similar functionality is integrated into some IDEs or can be added using additional plug-ins.

If tools are available, they should definitely be used within every project. They change the way people develop software. Common refactorings can be extremely smooth and simple using the tools. The renaming of a method that is used across hundreds of different locations within the system is just one click away. Refactorings are carried out far more often since these tools have been integrated into the IDEs. [Refactoring] gives a good overview of the available tools and extensive information on the topic.

Recommendations

- Do not believe in 'Never change a running system'!

- Make refactoring into an attitude so that you cannot imagine programming without it.

- Use a version control system with an optimistic locking mechanism.

- Break down large changes into small refactorings. Continually look for strategies for breaking down changes.

- Plan which refactorings are necessary and in which order they are used to carry out a large change.

- Always carry out refactorings that are oriented towards the goals of the users and customers. Refactoring is not an end in itself.

- Read the whole of [Fowler 99] and use it as a handbook for refactoring.

- Enhance your ideas for refactoring by reading [Kerievsky 02].

Reference to other XP practices

- *Metaphor*: A system with clear metaphors for your system also has an architectural framework that defines the boundaries within which refactorings can operate. This guarantees that you do not degrade the architecture by applying many small refactorings.

- *Collective ownership*: In an XP project, all developers are responsible for the system. If a developer notices a problem or something he does not like, he immediately eliminates it, even if the code did not come from him in the first place.

- *Testing*: Only if sufficient coverage is guaranteed with unit tests can refactoring be carried out. The unit tests do not guarantee that refactoring will not create undesirable side effects, but they considerably reduce the risk of them. They act as a safeguard.

- *Pair programming*: Unit tests help to maintain consistency during refactoring. If programming is carried out in pairs, there is an additional parallel code review and the danger of undesirable side effects is reduced even further. Pair programming also helps to break down larger refactorings as well as the execution planning of small refactorings.

- *Continuous integration*: Smaller refactorings favour continuous integration. Version control systems with optimistic locking strategies force small refactorings.

- *Simple design*: The guideline of implementing the simplest solution provides clear direction for the aim of refactoring. A refactoring is only meaningful if it simplifies the design. A clear distinction has to be made here between refactoring and further development. If the system is developed alongside the requirements of the users and customers, a simple design sometimes has to be made a bit more complicated in order to be able to cover the new requirements. In subsequent refactorings, the system can then be simplified again.

- *Sustainable pace*: If you carry out small refactorings and protect them through unit tests, you have an operational system available at any time. You can therefore go home when your working day is over. You do not need to stay for a few hours longer to get the system running again. By using refactoring, you can make sure that your system always retains an architecture that can be changed easily and that the cost of changes during the course of the development remains almost constant. You therefore do not run the danger of estimating incorrectly for a requirement and do not need to try to reconcile disappointed customers with overtime.

2.8 Pair programming

Description

Pair programming means that two developers regularly sit in front of a computer and work together. There is no division of tasks between them. Both developers are on equal terms. They discuss and work together on possible solutions and then implement them.

The fundamental idea behind pair programming is that reviews are good, both at a code level and a design level. Therefore we do them all the time; the easiest and simplest way to achieve this is to let the developers talk directly while sitting in front of the code. We consider pair programming as the *four eye principle*[7] in the development of software.

---

7. The four eye principle is used mainly in bank organisations. An employee makes a decision or creates or changes a document. Then a second person (often the head of the department or a colleague) takes a look at the decision or results of the work. This typically reduces the error rate. A German proverb says, 'Four eyes see more than two eyes'.

Of course, two developers cannot use the same keyboard at the same time: the keyboard has to be passed between the two developers. We can therefore distinguish between two roles: there is the developer with the mouse and keyboard who writes the code to solve a problem and explains to his partner what he is doing and why. The second developer assesses the solution of the first developer and thinks about simplifications, new test cases, alternative ways of solving the problem, design alternatives, refactoring, etc. You can consider the former as a pilot and the latter as a co-pilot, but the division of roles is not fixed. It varies all the time. It is particularly desirable that the roles (and, therefore, the keyboard and mouse) are frequently and easily swapped. The two programming partners should be equal.

Figure 2.3 Pair programming, seen through the eyes of a child (many thanks to Anna Wolf)

Experiences

Fewer computers We like to stress the fact, in particular to managers, that a software development company has to spend less money on computers as two people always sit in front of the same computer these days! OK, this is a joke, but we actually need fewer computers than developers. The need for high-performance computers with large monitors is decreasing in particular, since many of the activities that are done alone, such as writing short texts and reading and answering e-mail, can use less powerful computers with smaller monitors, or notebooks.

Since 1999, for the development of the JWAM framework and in other projects that run for more than a month, we have been using pair programming and we feel that our quality has improved considerably. We are more effective and our developers have a lot of fun in their work. The effects that are created by pair programming cannot only be seen internally, as our customers are also pleasantly happy.

Truck factor   Kent Beck introduces the concept of the truck factor (see [Beck 00]), which indicates the probability that a software project will fail if a team member is run over by a truck. A truck factor of 1.0 means that there is a 100% chance that the project will fail if, for example, the database specialist or the only team member who knows about a certain important area of the project drops out. Apart from large lorries, our developers have relatively few enemies but we are thinking about long-term illnesses, accidents, hard-working head hunters, and sudden relationship or career moves. How can pair programming help us?

This is typically the point at which many developers and project managers stand up and argue against it: 'No-one could know everything. We need specialists!' Of course, for any software development project, it is a blessing if there are experts with experience of the practices that are to be used. It is also certain that, with today's wealth of technologies, no individual developer can master everything up to expert level. We do, however, want to spread the special knowledge throughout the project team. Pair programming is well-suited to this because the experts teach the required details to another team member. This team member and the expert then work with the other team members the following day and spread this knowledge. It is not just a question of passing on the technical knowledge; pair programming also gives rise to a strong feeling of collective ownership. In classical development projects, components of the system are developed by different team members and a developer cannot change, or even understand, the components developed by other developers. In one project, we had to get by without our colleague Henning Wolf (project manager and architect) for nine weeks due to a slipped disc. It may have damaged his ego, but we managed to do it without any problems!

Net programming time   Developers are normally very stressed-out people. Imagine that you are sitting at your computer and want to implement a ground-breaking method, when the telephone rings. Shortly after the conversation with the customer, a friend rings up. He has come home after a long holiday in the USA and has a lot to tell you. You eventually sit back at your computer and a small symbol flashes on the monitor to indicate that there is e-mail waiting for you. You take a quick look at it and maybe even write an answer. It occurs to you that the stress of your job is worthwhile and that you have been able to invest a lot of money on the stock exchange – it is good that you have an Internet connection and can quickly look at what is going on.

This little story is not completely unrealistic and we know from our own experience that sometimes it is easy to be distracted. Pair programming helps in fighting distraction, because you make telephone calls (in particular, private calls) drastically shorter if someone is waiting for you. You also do not read e-mail whilst someone is sitting right next to you, not to mention looking at a Web site with your stock exchange quotations (maybe with the exception of the rates for your own company). In short, pair programming increases the concentration on tasks and the other activities of the normal working day have to be done at another time. It is helpful to agree on half an hour, for example, in the morning, at midday and in the evening when people can take care of e-mails, memos, travel expenses, etc.

At this point, it should be said that increased concentration goes hand in hand with increased effort. A day spent programming in a pair is considerably more exhausting than a day sat alone at a computer. Therefore we put great value on the pair taking sufficient breaks, which are useful for relaxing, normally alone, as well as for reflection about the work that has just been done or for thinking about the design for tasks that are still to be completed.

Training   Our own experience is confirmed in a study carried out by Laurie Williams (see [Williams 00]): pair programming is an excellent way of conveying practical knowledge, a good programming style, and experiences. In a pair, all that is required for things to work is an 'old hand' working with a less-experienced developer. This method of training is however sometimes quite exhausting for both partners. Two less-experienced developers have a steep learning curve in pair programming. We put this down to the fact that in pairs you give a lot of explanation of your motives, why you are arranging something in that way and not in another way, etc. It is a popular view that you have only really understood something correctly if you can explain it to someone else.

More unified code   However, the point must also be made that although the training of developers during pair programming is effective, the more experienced developer may be held back. Nevertheless, despite the training, the experienced developer produces usable results.

The number of programming errors and therefore also the number of program defects have reduced greatly since we started to program in pairs. The code we have produced since then looks much better, contains fewer defects, and is more understandable. We have also observed an increase in productivity during the programming itself: a reduction in syntax errors ensure that classes, as a rule, can be compiled at the first attempt.

Overall, the tendency we observed in non-XP projects to reduce the quality of the code if the deadline is close is not as pronounced when programming in pairs. There is always someone who makes sure that the test classes are still being written and that the variables are being named correctly.

Team size   Our experience has convinced us that pair programming produces a result of much better quality with the same cost. Previously, we were of the opinion that no more than eight to ten developers should work on a development project, otherwise the communication within the team becomes more difficult and the project is more difficult to manage. We do not know of any successful projects that were considerably larger than this. Larger project tasks should preferably be divided up into smaller ones and therefore into several projects. Thanks to the good communication between developers in pair programming with changing pairs, these days we would get involved with larger projects, with up to 16 developers programming in pairs.

Switching the *keyboard*   After three years' experience, we still do not have total control over a problem about which many colleagues who use pair programming complain: the keyboard is not switched between the developers often enough. We have always switched every 15 to 30 minutes, but we would like it to be done even more often. The problem is that the pilot is used to typing and does not offer the keyboard to the co-pilot often enough if he has an idea and is explaining it. This problem frequently occurs if there is a difference in the status or technical abilities of the two developers. The less qualified of the two does not simply take the keyboard himself. In our opinion, it is the task of the experienced developer to offer him the keyboard. The switching of the keyboard at fixed time intervals does not seem to us to make much sense, you should not carry out the switch too dogmatically. We are very happy with the results that we have produced in pairs but know that we can improve them even more.

How many pairs in *a room?*   Many people (most of them without any XP experience) say that it must be particularly loud in the office if there are several programming pairs working together. This is sometimes true. Despite this, a number of programming teams can work in the same room without disturbing one another. There should be agreement that the programmers do not talk loudly to one another. We have had surprisingly good experiences with up to five pairs in one small office. When the tasks are divided and the pairs begin their work in the morning, it is loud, occasionally very loud, but after a few minutes the volume regulates itself to an acceptable level. The room should not be too small, however; three pairs in an office of approximately eight square metres was one of our less pleasant experiences. In this case, the pairs sit too close to one another and the level of noise is constantly high.

Our experience, and that of other members of the XP community, is that it is important for all developers in a project team sit together in the same room, if possible. Communication works much better within one room than if I have to walk around the corner to speak to a colleague. It can also be important that the co-pilots half listen to what the others are talking about. If they do this, the teams can quickly clear up misunderstandings or can spot and avoid functional overlap at an early stage.

When we started programming in pairs, there were significant problems with the furnishings in our office. A desk with a set of drawers on one side allows only one person to sit at it. The second person then sits in front of the drawers and cannot put their legs under the table. Because of this, the second developer normally sits behind the first and is a lot further away. Also, a fast switch of the keyboard is not possible because the developers have to change sides each time. If the desks or drawers are dismantled, improved and more equal work can take place. Even worse than this are L-shaped desks that have the computer in the corner, as shown in Figure 2.4. These kinds of desks are not helpful and should be thrown away.[8]

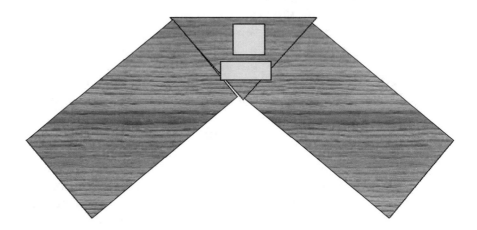

Figure 2.4 Unsuitable: L-shaped desk arrangement

Often we use a seating arrangement such as that shown in Figure 2.5 and sit at the corner of a normal table without drawers. The leg of the table divides the areas of the developers and there is very little disruption.

8. One reviewer of this book reported to us that it is possible to sit at such a desk in a way that enables both partners to sit equally in front of the keyboard. This can only work on the long side of the desk and not within the bend.

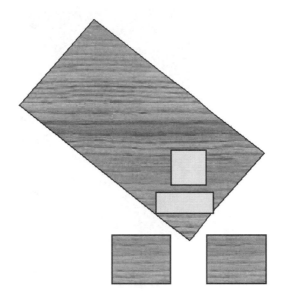

Figure 2.5   More suitable: Computer in the corner

However, we can imagine that a rounded corner, such as that shown in Figure 2.6, would be better, with a leg that was attached further under the table.

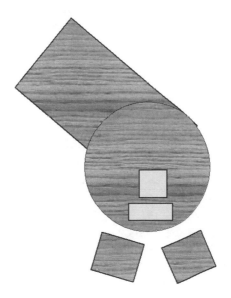

Figure 2.6   Optimal: Round table for pair programming

Figure 2.7 An example from our office

The position of the computer is also important. Switching the keyboard should be possible without having to make big changes to the seating plan or position. In Figure 2.7, you can see that the developer on the left is sitting crookedly in his chair. This makes it more difficult to switch the keyboard as he has to change the way he is sitting in order to be able to type on the keyboard in an upright position. In principle, we want to point out that it is a poor excuse if pair programming is not applied because the furniture is not suitable! It can be organised anywhere, if you really want it.

Soft skills   Pair programming certainly makes more demands on the individual than is normal in training. Many of our colleagues found it hard to accept criticism at the beginning. With our communication abilities, we have had hardly any difficulties in our own company but we know from other projects that it can lead to problems.

In our opinion, it is important that the whole team understands that a task is everyone's responsibility and is measured on how successful it is. 'No one person in the team is better than any other' is an ideal that the team should constantly work to. Working with trust in one another, without disagreements and discussions to the bitter end makes work easier for everyone.

It is our experience that conflict and communication skills are not only necessary for developers in pair programming. When working with customers, these skills also play an important role.

We have discussed pair programming with many developers from other companies and organisations. We constantly meet sceptics who have not actually tried it out or have categorically turned it down, but we also meet colleagues who think that pair programming slows them down. This discussion is made more intense by the question of whether programming in pairs or programming alone is quicker. We will not take this discussion to the end here, but want to give our personal opinion: in terms of productivity, we suspect that pair programming gives a slight gain, due to the increase of the net programming time. In terms of quality, we feel that the benefits of the introduction of pair programming have been more than obvious.

Lone fighters

Anyone who, like us, is convinced by pair programming may be concerned by the question of what should be done if one or several employees do not want to work pairs. This is a problem because, in an organisational context, a lone fighter is very difficult to integrate into a team that is programming in pairs. Pair programming, as described above, is used for regular reviews and requires all team members to have knowledge of the system.

If we had known what we know now, we would have done without one employee in a project. Too few alternatives and altogether too few resources for the projects did not allow for this decision. In such cases, it is appropriate that the code of the individual developers is systematically examined. This does however require another employee to be available to carry out the examination. We also have tried giving the individual developer simple tasks, which complicates the planning. In retrospect, even the supposedly simple tasks of the quality of the interfaces and the code would have been better created in pairs.

We occasionally find a situation in which there is an odd number of developers in a project team. We then make sure that no developer has to work alone for more than half a day. This is also necessary because most of our colleagues are so used to programming in pairs that they no longer like programming alone. We have made an interesting observation: programmers who usually program in pairs also produce better code when they sit alone at a computer. We suspect that the stronger project culture is the reason for this. This observation cannot be made in the case of programmers who permanently work alone.

Recommendations

- You have to learn how to program in pairs. Eight hours working in a pair are much more exhausting than eight hours working alone. So take it easy!

- During the learning process, give feedback about what was good and not so good.

- Make, or if necessary force, a lot of breaks.

- Limit discussions about concepts during the programming.

- Move to another place (e.g. the cafeteria) when taking a break.

- Do not check e-mails, stock quotations or telephone calls when programming in pairs.

- Keep interruptions to a minimum.

- Pair programming is suitable for routine and mass changes.

- Management must be explicit that they want pair programming.

- A faster PC and a larger monitor (19-inch, as a minimum) are important.

- Make leg room: there must not be any fixed containers on the sides of the tables.

- Changing roles (switching the keyboard) has to be as easy as possible.

- A separation between the work place and the development PC is sensible.

- The keyboard should be switched several times an hour.

- If an employee does not want to program in pairs, remove him from the team. If you cannot do this, review intensively the code produced in isolation, make programming in pairs more acceptable and look for a replacement for this developer.

Reference to other XP practices

- *Collective ownership:* Pair programming encourages the common perception of ownership. The knowledge about the construction of the system and details about certain parts of the system are spread rapidly throughout the team, especially if the pairs are well mixed up and swapped.

- *Simple design:* Whilst working alone, a developer all too often stocks up on technology. The second developer of a pair helps to choose a solution that is easier and quicker to implement and completely sufficient. 'Four eyes design better than two.'

- *Testing:* In most software development projects, testing is inexcusably neglected. Pair programming promotes the test-driven process through an increase in programming discipline.

- *Coding standards:* The increase in discipline in the work of two people promotes compliance to standards. It is clear to every developer that his code is seen by others.

- *Continuous integration:* The general planning of programming tasks in pairs promotes a breakdown of programming into smaller steps so that results can be integrated continuously.

- *Refactoring:* As well as determining places in the source code that need to be revised, planning of occasionally quite complicated refactoring is considerably easier with two people.

- *Metaphor:* During pair programming, two people have the same idea of a suitable design in their minds. Behind this there is a vivid picture of the system to be created. Developers with a similar background of design metaphors quickly work harmoniously.

- *Sustainable pace:* Pair programming is exhausting but successful. 40 hours a week are normally sufficient. Our experience shows that within these 40 hours a person will work more intensively than if they were working on their own and the project moves forward continuously.

2.9 Collective ownership

Description

In an XP project, all source code, documents, and components of the system that are created belong to the whole team. This means that anyone in the project can change any source code files or documents at any time. This of course only works completely if the members of the project have the same basic qualifications.

Similar levels of ability and

This results in the requirement that all members of the project have to have the same level of ability and knowledge. This requirement can be met if the members of the project who have more knowledge in one area 'train' the others. Thus you can achieve similar abilities while still using the special knowledge of members of the project.

No accusations　　Collective ownership also means that if there is a problem in the project, the whole team is always responsible. If, for example, there is an error in the application, tracing it back to the 'originator' would be very time-consuming, if not impossible, and is unnecessary. The person who finds out about the error removes it as soon as possible. This distinguishes the collective ownership of XP projects from 'no ownership'. If no one feels responsible for a part of the system, necessary changes will be put off or ignored. If collective ownership is consistently practised, the truck factor (see Section 2.8) can be lowered considerably.

Truck factor　　As described here, the components, code and documents are owned collectively by the development team; users have other responsibilities.

Experiences

Loss of employees　　In pair programming, collective ownership is enhanced by changing pairs. Knowledge about the project can be so well-distributed throughout the team that the loss of an employee would hardly be noticed. In Section 2.8., we mentioned a project in which a team of three developers lost one of its key players for nine weeks because of a slipped disc. This did not lead to any difficulties in the project. The other two developers were able to carry on with the project during this time with no problems.

In another project, the developer managing the project was required in another project. There was an extremely short hand-over time (1 day) between this developer and his successor. As expected, this change caused a lot of temporary irritation for the customer. However, the irritations stopped after a few days and the progress of the project was hardly affected by the exchange of developers as the other members of the project had enough knowledge of the whole project.

Differing levels of ability and knowledge　　We have been part of projects in which people with different levels of ability and knowledge worked together. Organisation developers, users, database administrators and developers were involved. Of course, in such projects we do not strive for all members of the project to be equal in all areas: teaching programming to users does not make sense. In these cases, we only standardise the levels of ability and knowledge within the separate groups. If the project includes group of people with disparate abilities and knowledge, the need for communication in the team increases even further. The groups may have a tendency to isolate themselves. Suitable means (e.g. daily brief status meetings and social events) must be used to ensure that communication between the groups does not break down. Individual project tasks should be spread out so that members from all groups are involved.

Unfortunately, in many projects this does not happen. Task areas are filled according to ability or knowledge: the organisation developers describe the business processes and how the software is to look; the database administrators design the data model; and the developers write the programs. This kind of division creates unnecessary friction between the groups and generates a waterfall-like development process.

Levelling may be a long job. If, for example, a Java project contains developers with five years' experience of object-oriented programming and developers who have only just learnt object-orientation and Java, the difference in ability and knowledge can persist for years. Standardisation in the project would not be possible. The aim, however, must always be to reduce the differences in ability.

Geographical differences

The spatial division of project members can also play a role. If, for example, two groups are separated by more than one door or a floor, our experience is that they are less likely to communicate with one another. If the team, on the other hand, sits in a large room or in several rooms that are directly connected, this promotes cooperation.

With collective ownership, the results of a developer are open to assessment and change by others taking part in the project. For some developers, this is a gigantic psychological hurdle. They may be scared that another developer will 'ruin' their work or it may emerge that they are not as outstanding as they themselves or others think.

If such problems occur, they should be dealt with sensitively. We would not, however, make any concessions to developers. If they cannot get used to collective ownership, we would remove them from the project or, at least, not use them in future projects.

Part-time workers

A developer may not be available to a project 100% of the time; for example, the developer may be working on several projects at the same time. If possible, developers should not work on several projects at the same time but this cannot always be avoided. In such cases, collective ownership helps because the other developers do not have to wait for those who are not available. It is also possible to integrate employees who do not have full-time posts without causing any problems.

Version control

Version control is more important to the implementation of collective ownership than in conventional development projects. A professional version control system can be used or version control can be simulated. If, for example, we work collectively on a text document, then we copy the document before we make a change. The file name of the copy contains the date of the change and the identification code of the author, so that it is easy to tell who worked on which document last, in the file system. If the date is coded in the form Year-Month-Day, the most recent document is shown first in lexical sorting. Incidentally, this is how we worked when writing this book.

Simulated version management is certainly not always the best alternative. Even working on a book can be implemented very elegantly with a version management system (for example, CS-RCS) which allows Diff and Merge functionality on Word files. We recommend that you follow the XP principle that the simplest solution is often the best.

Recommendation

• Strive for standardisation of abilities and knowledge in the project.

• If people with different abilities and knowledge are involved in the project, distribute the tasks evenly between them.

• Make sure that the members of the project work as closely to one another as possible. Ten or more people in a room is no problem if they are all working on the same project. To achieve this, make sure you are flexible: if you have adjustable walls, adjust them; use the redirection functions of your telephone system to enable employees to transfer their telephone number on to their new workplace.

• Use a version control system for your source code and all other documents in the project. Make sure that the version control system is up to the job. A version control system that is difficult to master sometimes causes more harm.

• Introduce collective ownership to projects that are already running and where collective ownership is not yet implemented.

Reference to other XP practices

• *Pair programming*: Pair programming facilitates collective ownership since two developers are responsible for creating source code. Pair programming is very difficult unless it is combined with collective ownership. If there is no collective ownership, the source code always 'belongs' to one of the two programmers and the partners are no longer equal.

• *Refactoring*: Refactoring should be carried out as soon as it is needed, by someone who sees the need for the refactoring. If the 'owners' of source code must always be asked to carry out a refactoring, unnecessary friction arises in the project.

- *Testing*: In the case of collective ownership, developers are sometimes scared that other developers can 'damage' their source code because they have not understood it correctly. If, however, the source code is protected with unit tests, this risk is considerably reduced. Each developer can do anything, as long as it does not fail the tests. It is malicious to change the source code and then delete the unit test so that the source code does not fail the test.

- *Coding standards*: If the source code is always formatted in a uniform way, the developer cannot be recognised from the format of the source code. Moreover, it is easier for developers to find their way around unfamiliar source code. Developers do not then succumb to the temptation of reformatting unfamiliar source code according to their own preferences before they change it.

- *Continuous integration*: Continuous integration facilitates collective ownership because every developer can quickly see and use all of the changes. If any developer can change any source code at any time, the probability of conflicts increases at first. Continuous integration of modified source code reduces the probability of conflict.

2.10 Continuous integration

Description

In an extreme programming project, a team of developers work on a software system. All developers in the process are equal and any developer can change any piece of code in the system (see Section 2.9).

In order to support this and to make small releases possible, modified source has to be uncomplicated, integrated and quickly accessible to other developers. XP prescribes the practice of continuous integration, in which small changes to the source code are made accessible to other developers on an integration machine (see Section 2.5).

Integration machine The integration machine is a computer that is used solely for the integration of new source. If a pair of developers check in new code, unit tests for the whole system are run on the integration machine. If all tests are successful, the integration is successful and the developers may leave their changes on the integration machine. If the tests do not run successfully, the developers are responsible for rolling the whole system back to an error-free status. Their work on the integration computer is only complete if either they have integrated their changes and carried out all tests successfully or they have deleted their changes from the integration machine and the system runs all the unit tests again.

The integration machine therefore makes sure that at any time there is an operational and tested version of the whole system. Moreover, this procedure defines clear responsibilities: only if all unit tests are running can the developers leave the integration machine. Consequently, each developer is responsible for passing the system on in an error-free state and can, on the other hand, rely on finding the integration machine with the system in an operational state.

In order to keep the work on the integration machine simple and to make changes accessible to other developers as quickly as possible, the changes should be small. By making them small, simple integrations are possible. Other developers in the team can immediately profit from this and the risk of a clash in development is minimised. At the same time, the expense of joining different branches of development is reduced.

Continuous integration takes place as the 'nightly build'. With continuous integration, developers get immediate feedback about the whole system and can see whether their changes harmonise with the remainder of the system.

Experiences

Continuous integration has proved successful in our development projects. The team development is supported particularly well by continuous integration and it makes it possible to work on the same goal with many pairs at the same time.

As a guideline, the XP community has set the minimum as one integration per day, per pair of developers. It does not always make sense to leave non-integrated changes on a development computer overnight. We recommend that you carry out 10–20 integrations per day across the team. Our experience shows that this is an achievable goal and can even be exceeded. In a project with seven developers we sometimes achieve 20 integrations or more per day.

Source code management Continuous integration requires a suitable environment underpinned by a source code control system or a version control system. These tools have become established for the development of software in teams but can lead to problems with continuous integration. The question of when source code can be processed is important: if small changes are to be made quickly, all sources always have to be accessible and, above all, changeable. The work on a problem cannot be hindered or delayed because someone has acquired exclusive access to the required source. If you use a version control system in which sources are locked for processing, the work is hindered and additional need for coordination arises. In such projects, it is often the case that a developer must process source code that is locked by another developer. It is particularly problematic if the co-worker leaves the office without releasing the source again, either because his work is not yet complete or because he has forgotten to do so. Normally, optimistic locking strategies are used in tight team development and our experience shows that it is precisely these strategies that we require for continuous integration. Each pair of developers can change, at their development PC, any source that is necessary for the solution of the current task. If source code is changed by two pairs at the same time, the changes must be combined ('merged') in the integration. If the integration steps are small enough, this occurs only rarely. In our professional XP projects, this kind of conflict is extremely rare and there are few problems when merging changes, in particular because they are small and normally local. Also, from time to time the developers coordinate their work by talking to each other about parallel changes. This supplements the continuous integration in an uncomplicated way.

Smaller refactorings   As a particularly positive effect of continuous integration, over a long period of development we have established that refactoring changes become smaller. The developers plan and implement small changes that can be integrated in isolation from each other. The risk of larger, more problematic changes is consequently minimised. Frequent refactorings occur not only because it is predetermined or recommended by XP, and the developers keep to the guidelines, but also because they try to prevent having to merge modified sources. During integration, the development pair is obliged to guarantee an operational status on the integration machine. If another pair has in the meantime changed the same sources, integration becomes more complicated, since the pair has to combine the changes; it is not simply a case of copying the individual sources any more. Nobody likes doing this work and, of course, the faster a pair integrates, the lower the risk that this merge has to be carried out. When working in sprints (see Section 5.4), from time to time there is even a certain playful competition to integrate faster than co-workers who may have changed the same sources.[9] Continuous integration should not mean that you only integrate in order to be faster than the other developers; however, this experience shows that working in teams leads to smaller changes and faster integration cycles.

---

9. We would not like to create the impression here that a competition for the quickest integration is desirable. This would not correspond to the XP philosophy. By the way, the easier the merge effort is made by the use of appropriate merge tools, the less competition there is.

Size of changes   If we talk about 'small' changes in this context, we generally mean the effort that is connected to this change. For example, if we want to change a package structure, many source files are involved but the change can be made in a few minutes. This is a small change and can be done in one step. Larger changes mean a lot of effort and should be broken down. In Section 2.7 we discussed in detail why and how you can break down changes.

Recommendations

- Think about whether a physical integration machine should be used or whether a virtual integration server via a version control system is sufficient.

- Choose the integration tools with care! Do not throw XP ideas overboard in the process: decide on either a specific XP tool (for example, the JWAM IntegrationServer) or a simple version control tool that can be extended by appropriate conventions.

- Establish conventions for integration if you employ a simple version control system. For example, each developer is only allowed to check in if all tests are running on his computer and he has an up-to-date version of the unchanged sources. In addition, all unit tests must be carried out on a reference machine at regular intervals to prevent problems arising that are specific to the development environment.

Reference to other XP practices

- *Refactoring*: You can improve existing code by refactoring. Refactorings should be processed in small steps and made accessible to other developers quickly. Continuous integration is the ideal way of doing this. Furthermore, we have seen that continuous integration encourages developers to carry out refactoring in smaller steps.

- *Collective ownership*: Each developer can make changes to the source at any time. Continuous integration enables developers to make their changes available quickly. This minimises the risk that a piece of code will be produced by several developers at once. At the same time, other developers profit from changes extremely quickly.

- *Small releases*: After every integration, a completely operational version of the system is available. One can almost say that an up-to-date release can be copied from the integration server at any time.

- *Testing*: Continuous integration requires test cases. After an integration using the appropriate tools, it can be proven that the system still works. This helps to define responsibilities clearly.

- *Pair programming*: The number of threads of development are reduced by programming in pairs, since two developers work on a problem. This also reduces the danger of having to bring together mutual changes during an integration.

- *Coding standards*: Continuous integration is based on the idea of developers replacing and developing source code. This is only meaningful if there are appropriate coding standards. If coding standards do not exist, developers are less happy to carry out changes to unfamiliar source code.

2.11 Coding standards

Description

Coding standards establish the external form of the source code. They determine, for example, in which form curly braces should be inserted into a Java program, at which points there should be spaces, and in which form comments are put into the code. Coding standards also include scripts, commonly used development environments, keyboard assignments, short-cuts, and other tools that make programming easier.

If a team has these kinds of coding standards, the source code will look uniform. The immediate advantage is that developers do not have to get used to a different layout if they read a piece of code and want to understand something that was created by another programmer. As a rule, you can test the success of a programming standard by seeing how far the author can be identified from the external form of the code. You should not be able to do this in XP projects. Coding standards also make pair programming is a lot easier since no one has to get used to the individual programming environment of a co-worker.

Experiences

If we want to develop software in a team, and we can hardly imagine anything else in today's software development environment, there must be guidelines for how the source code looks. Otherwise, it will be increasingly difficult for the developers to find their way around source code written by other developers.

We rarely find a situation in which a team of software developers has no coding standards. In such cases, there is a culture of individualists and experts and collective ownership is a foreign word. As a rule, coding standards are defined and used, and we find it difficult to imagine working without explicit coding standards. This is the only way for a team to operate with collective ownership. If there are no standards, many developers find it difficult and time-consuming to read code written by someone else. People will be reluctant to change a piece of code if they must make a great effort to find their way around. If a feeling of uncertainty dominates the developer and he feels uneasy, it will be contrary to the idea of collective ownership and team development is made extremely difficult.

Creating and using coding standards   The JWAM framework comes with coding standards. We first defined a set of guidelines that guarantee a uniform appearance of the source code. The developer should not have to read an extensive collection of guidelines. If the coding standards consist of more than ten pages, they are put aside rather than taken to heart. Sample source code has proved particularly useful for providing guidelines: it illustrates the guidelines and can also be used as the template for source code.

Sun Microsystems has provided coding standards for Java, which determine quite extensively the format of Java source code (see http://www.javasoft.com). These standards can be used as they are but, in our view, you do not need to shy away from adapting such standards to your own needs.

We have adapted the standards to include extensions and modifications for a specific project. It is sensible to work with the accepted standards and change or extend them if you need to. For example, we have introduced special meta tags for the use of 'Design by Contract' (see [Meyer 97]). The original Sun standards do not contain them since Design by Contract is not a fixed component of the Java language. These additional meta tags are similar to the existing meta tags for JavaDoc, so that they are easy for a practised Java programmer to understand, even if he does not use Design by Contract.

The way in which we format curly braces also deviates from the Sun guidelines. We always put an open curly brace on a new line and never at the end of a program text line. This change may appear to be marginal and petty, but we chose this formatting before Sun released guidelines and we still feel that it is clearer. We have discussed at some length the option of bringing our guidelines into line with those of Sun, but in the end we decided against it: the change would have meant great interference in the existing code and would have not been profitable. In such a case, one should have the courage to deviate from the standard. This is not to say that set coding standards should never be changed again. Quite the contrary: if a guideline turns out to be difficult or even nonsensical, it should be changed even if a considerable amount of code has to be changed. It is better to invest this effort than to work with impractical coding standards. If the developers think the coding standards are unusable or impractical, they tend not to implement them and uncontrolled growth arises. You should avoid this danger, even if you have to change the guidelines.

If you currently do not use coding standards, you should not waste too much time creating them. Discussions about coding standards can get out of control. Do not waste your time with unfruitful discussions in which details are chewed over for hours. If you are in doubt, simply use available standards, such as Sun's Java Coding Conventions.

Collective programming environment In addition to source code standards, we have formed a standard for the programming environment over the course of time. We have not written about it, but we have evolved an environment that has proved to be particularly useful for programming in pairs.

Recommendations

- Formulate coding standards in the imperative! This makes the guidelines clear and easy to understand.

- Do not make the coding standards too long. Avoid making them more than ten pages.

- Enrich the coding standards with sample source code. It will facilitate the familiarisation and is clearer than lengthy text.

- Do not discuss coding standards for too long. When in doubt, use a set of guidelines that already exist (for example, the Java Code Conventions or the JWAM Styleguides).

- Have the courage to change existing coding standards. Nothing is worse than having defined an unusable standard which nobody, understandably enough, sticks to.

- Tools can help you compress existing source code into a standard. This also makes it easier to change a coding standard. JIndent and the IDEA programming environment contain this functionality. These tools do not, unfortunately, take care of everything (for example, they do not support Design by Contract).

Reference to other XP practices

- *Collective ownership*: Collective ownership is made considerably more difficult if there are no coding standards. It is much easier to change a piece of code if its external appearance is familiar. If developers have to invest a lot of time in learning to read the code, team development is slowed down and is made more difficult.

- *Pair programming*: Coding standards have a twofold effect when programming in pairs. During programming, the partner naturally makes sure that the coding standards are being adhered to. Standards also make collective programming easier: a developer does not have to spend half his time following the different style of his partner. He can concentrate fully on the content of the program. Discussions between developers about the formatting of the source code are also minimised.

- *Continuous integration*: The connection between standards and continuous integration is not so obvious. It is true that small changes and refactoring are simplified by coding standards. However, these arguments can be ascribed to collective ownership, which we see as the main connection.

2.12 Sustainable pace

Description

It seems hardly necessary to engage in a serious discussion about why it is sensible for software developers not to work more than 40 hours a week. Despite this, for many software developers the reality looks different. In particular, consultants are frequently put into projects that have a fixed deadline, which can allegedly only be kept by means of overtime. One can only ask who sets such deadlines and on what basis? Regular overtime is an indication of poor management of the development process. However, there are managers who believe that a 60 hour week is perfectly normal and therefore expect the same input from their developers.

Don't work longer, work better!

The present lack of qualified software developers is often used as the grounds for overtime. When all is said and done, overtime is counterproductive because developers who are constantly overloaded with work tend to suffer from illness and are less productive. Eventually, they become dissatisfied and hand in their notice to an employer who demands overtime. On the other hand, there are developers who deliberately work overtime in order to earn more money. This may make sense if that is what they want to do, but an employer should not make this a permanent situation, for the reasons mentioned above.

Experiences

We interpret constant overtime in a project as a symptom of problems in a development process. Of course, our projects also have phases in which the whole team does overtime. Software development projects have these so-called 'hot phases', but they should not last longer than two to three weeks. It makes no sense to complete a project in a hurry. Most customers and users would prefer a high-quality system more than a system that was ready when the deadline arrived, even if they would prefer to have both. If overtime is due to weaknesses in the management, the project owners may not have the courage to admit to the customers that the project is delayed.[10] If you have built up a good relationship with the customer, he will tolerate any delay that is reported early, in our experience. Users have also learnt that there are always imponderables in software development projects.

When the authors discussed the 40-hour week for the first time, we were convinced that it could not work. There were a number of reasons for this:

- XP projects are extremely goal-oriented and success-oriented, and the achievement of goals and success does not stop at a 40-hour limit.

- XP projects deliver smaller system versions as frequently as possible. This means, however, that there is constantly a looming deadline in which the program has promised functionality. Should developers go home after 40 hours or should they achieve the promised functionality?

- We find that XP developers have a lot of fun when they are working and do not watch the clock.

A sample investigation of the time sheets of our co-workers brought to light that only the part-time workers and we authors do any overtime! Our full-time co-workers only occasionally work overtime, due to journey time, if the customer is far away. Our part-timers are obviously all flexible enough to work more than the agreed part-time. They are also motivated by their own interest in successful projects and project progress.

We estimate that the fact that full-time workers do so little overtime is connected to the use of XP practices. Through pair programming, small releases, continuous integration, etc. the work is very intense. In a week

---

10. That is, not all story cards for the next release can be implemented in this iteration.

with 40 working hours, considerably more work is carried out than is normal in other projects. So that this intensity can work, a couple of additional rules are necessary:

- Make a distinction between programming time, administration time, and breaks.

- Do not read your e-mails and do not check share prices during programming time.

- Do not talk to your partner about irrelevant things during the programming time.

- Take many short breaks. Our rule of thumb says that you should take a 15-minute break in every 60 to 90 minutes.

- In the breaks, relax just as intensively as you work during the programming time.

- Do not take a break at your computer. Deliberately change the location.

- Take care of e-mails etc. during planned administration time. This work is not done in pairs. Carry out administration at a time that does not fall into highly creative phases. This creativity is required for programming.

- Make sure that, on average, there is no more than one hour of administration time per day. If more is necessary, there is a problem with the organisational structure. Clarify this with the supervisor responsible.

In our experience, willingness to do more work fundamentally depends on the culture of the company. Employees want to be asked if they want to do overtime; it should not be arranged on high and simply imposed. Also, the employees must be able to see that the company is serious when stating that they generally want to keep to the 40-hour week. This includes compensation in the form of money or free time for overtime worked. Last but not least, the success that is achieved through the overtime should be recognised as a success of the team and the individual employees.

Recommendations

- Get an overview of overtime that has been worked recently (e.g. in the last three months).

- Offer your employees compensation for overtime, but not just simply money!

- After an exhausting project with a lot of overtime, allow your developers one to two weeks to reflect on the work that was done. Your developers could use the time to get to know new technologies, APIs or frameworks (do you already know JWAM?).

- If eight hours a day are simply not sufficient for you or your developers, then once in a while go home on a Friday after half a day and have a well-earned and relaxing weekend.

- In general do not plan internal meetings, customer appointments, etc. for Fridays.

Reference to other XP practices

- *Small releases:* Create a regular light to moderately severe deadline for the entire team. This may occasionally stand contrary to the 40-hour week, but the features that are still incomplete can be contained in the next small release.

- *Simple design:* Always choosing the most simple possible solution makes it easier to keep to the 40-hour week, because simple solutions can be implemented a lot more quickly than complicated ones. We also think that keeping to an average of 40 hours per week is a precondition for being able to identify simple designs and solutions. Someone who is overworked lacks the necessary concentration to find the most simple solution.

- *Collective ownership, pair programming and the planning game:* Breaking tasks down into an XP development process (small, easily-understood tasks that can be worked on by everyone in the team) promote the 40-hour week. Through collective ownership and pair programming, the handling of tasks becomes independent of individuals (see also the Truck Factor in Section 2.8), which makes it possible for individuals to leave earlier. However, arrangements within a team and, in particular, in a pair must be sensible in order not to leave one programming partner unexpectedly alone for a time.

2.13 Literature

Apache Jakarta Project. *Ant.* http://jakarta.apache.org/ant/
This is a tool for Java that supports the application build process very well. Build scripts are expressed as XML and use a number of built-in functions.

Bäumer, Dirk, *et al.* 1997. 'Framework Development for Large Systems' in *Communications of the ACM*, 40(10).

Beck, Kent. 2000. *Extreme Programming Explained: Embrace change.* Reading, Massachusetts, Addison-Wesley.
This first book on XP is the benchmark for the topic. It gives a good overview of XP and the philosophy behind it. As an introduction, it is an absolute must.

Beck, Kent, and Fowler, Martin. 2000. *Planning Extreme Programming.* Reading, Massachusetts, Addison-Wesley.
The authors are at the centre of the XP movement and this book gives a detailed insight into the planning of XP projects. It highlights and discusses diverse aspects of project planning with and for XP.

CruiseControl. Open-source project at SourceForge, http://www.source-forge.net
CruiseControl is a system for combining version management systems and continuous integration. After every integration, it carries out the unit tests automatically and gives feedback about possible errors. The results can be viewed easily via a Web interface.

Fowler, Martin. 1999. *Refactoring: Improving the design of existing code.* Reading, Massachusetts, Addison-Wesley.
This book is the benchmark on the topic of refactoring, indispensable even for the experienced developer. It contains an extensive list of frequently required refactorings, with rationale, examples, and advice about the steps of refactoring.

Gamma, Erich, *et al.* 1996. *Design Pattern: Elements of reusable object-oriented software.* Bonn, Addison-Wesley.
This book has set the standard for design patterns and should be on the shelf of every object-oriented developer.

Hunt, Andrew, and Thomas, David. 1999. *The Pragmatic Programmer: From journeyman to master.* Addison-Wesley Longman. http://pragmaticprogrammer.com
This book is not about XP but it represents a similar philosophy. Many examples and analogies, such as the Broken Window theory, take a pragmatic approach to the development of software. This book should be in the library of every programmer.

Jeffries, Ron, Anderson, Ann, and Hendrickson, Chet. 2000. *Extreme Programming Installed.* Reading, Massachusetts, Addison-Wesley.
The members of the C3 project team[11] explain the concept of XP in detail and give the reader a number of hints and tips along the way.

JUnit Test Framework. http://www.junit.org
JUnit is a unit test framework for Java. It has been developed by Kent Beck and Erich Gamma and is very popular. As well as diverse articles, there are also a number of interesting extensions of JUnit, which allow, for example, unit tests to be written for Web applications or J2EE uses.

JWAM Framework, IT Workplace Solutions GmbH. http://www.jwam.org
This is a framework written in Java for interactive application systems that are developed according to the WAM metaphor (see [Züllighoven 02]). The JWAM framework itself is developed with the help of XP practices and is one of our largest XP projects.

Kerievsky, Joshua. 2002. *Refactoring to Patterns.*
This book (http://www.industriallogic.com/xp/refactoring/ has a pre-publication version) builds very well from the work of Martin Fowler. It describes a refactoring catalog based on refactoring descriptions that introduce common design patterns into existing software.

Mackinnon, Tim, Freeman, Steve, and Craig, Philip. 2000. 'Endo-Testing: Unit-Testing with Mock Objects' in Michele Marchesi and Giancarlo Succi (eds.), *Extreme Programming Examined.* Reading, Massachusetts, Addison-Wesley.
This book contains diverse, interesting articles, from the first XP conference, that shed light on different facets of XP and offer new suggestions.

---

11. The XP practices were used together for the first time in the C3 project.

Meyer, Bertrand. 1997. *Object-Oriented Software Construction*, second edition. Prentice Hall.

This highly recommended book explains all the basic concepts of object-orientation in impressive ways. In particular, the Open–Close and Design by Contract principles are highlights of this book.

Newkirk, James, and Martin, Robert C. 2001. *Extreme Programming in Practice*. Reading, Massachusetts, Addison-Wesley.

This book describes a relatively small but real project which was carried out with XP. The first iteration is described to the reader in detail and the authors evaluate critically the XP practices that they have used successfully. This is an interesting book for beginners but the experienced developer will not find much new here.

Optional Scope Contracts. http://www.XProgramming.com/xpublications.htm

The theme of this article is the form of contract for cyclic software development projects. Kent Beck and Dave Cleal argue that classical fixed-price projects determine the price, scope and deadline, allowing only the quality to vary. In contracts with variable extents, the price, deadline, and quality are firmly defined. The desired scope is written into the contract but can be varied during the course of the project.

Refactoring. http://www.refactoring.com/

Martin Fowler maintains this Web site, which gives a good overview of the topic of refactoring. It contains a number of useful links about the topic as well as corrections and additions to [Fowler 99].

Smalltalk Refactoring Browser. http://chip.cs.uiuc.edu/users/brant/Refactory/

The Smalltalk Refactoring Browser was the first tool to support automated refactoring and is still a valid model for refactoring support in programming environments.

Wiki. http://c2.com/cgi/wiki

Ward Cunningham maintains this Web site which enables the community to share information.

Williams, Laurie. 2000. Dissertation and other publications. http://pairprogramming.com

In his dissertation, Laurie Williams has carried out empirical investigations of XP and pair programming in particular. The investigations indicate that pair programming takes a lot more resources but produces much better results.

Wilson, James Q., and Kelling, George. 1982. 'Broken Windows: The police and neighborhood safety' in *The Atlantic Monthly*, 249(3):29–38. http://www.theatlantic.com/politics/crime/windows.htm
> *This article describes the Broken Window Theory and is the basis for the transfer to software development in [Hunt and Thomas 99]. Experiments in the Broken Window Theory can be traced back to Philip Zimbardo (see http://www.criminology.fsu.edu/crimtheory/zimbardo.htm)*

XPWeb, Extreme Programming Web site. http://www.xprogramming.com
> *On this Web site by Ron Jeffries, there are a number of interesting articles and links to test frameworks for every conceivable programming language.*

Züllighoven, Heinz. 2002. *The Object-Oriented Construction Handbook*. to be published by Morgen Kaufmann.
> *The basis of the Tools and Materials Approach are described in detail in this book. As well as the pure approach, there are also many design instructions and tips for developing software architectures and projects in the object-oriented environment.*

Roles

3

In this chapter we discuss the typical roles in an XP project. It is important to understand that one person can fill several roles and one role can be filled by several people. The starting point for this chapter is the roles described by Kent Beck (see [Beck 00]). We have adapted these roles on the basis of our project experiences: in particular, we now split up the XP customer roles into client and user roles.

3.1 Customer

The customer decides on what is to be programmed and when. Often, at the start of the project, the details of what has to be developed is not completely clear. In this context, software development is a learning process not only for the developer, but also for the customers. Customers and developers must learn which support from a system is possible and meaningful, if any. The customer can then define what is going to be developed and in what order.

According to XP, the customer should write story cards from their point of view. This is an important task since story cards describe the system to be built and act as the discussion material for the planning game. Programmers implement the stories defined by the customer. That does not mean that story cards have to contain everything, like a detailed specification. Story cards act as 'a promise of communication' between customer and developer. If anything is not clear about the story during the implementation, the programmer can ask the customer to explain the story in more detail. This is another responsibility of the customer – explaining what a story means.

Every story should contain an acceptance test that enables the story to be checked against some customer-defined criteria. A story must also be of such a size that it can be estimated by the programmers and implemented in one iteration. If not, the customer has to split or change the story.

As you can see, story cards are very important. Therefore, the customer has to learn how to write story cards. If the customer has never written story cards before, developers must prevent them from being unsatisfactory at the start of the project. The developers must then give the customers feedback and support their learning process.

The customer role within an XP project must be played by a responsible person. In contrast to many other kinds of software development projects the customer of an XP project has much more insight into the project and can influence and steer the project in a powerful way. The customer must use this power in a responsible way.

3.2 Programmer

It is clear that the programmers develop the system. In contrast to previous development processes (such as, for example, the waterfall model), programmers are not only responsible for coding, they also estimate and plan the development efforts and design, document and test the system.

The main development cycle has the following steps: estimate a story, divide the story into several tasks (using task cards, which are also written for technical tasks, such as refactoring, that improve the system architecture), implement the tasks for the story; and continue with the next story. If anything is unclear regarding the story or what the system should do, the developers should ask the customer.

During the implementation of a story the programmers develop features by looking at the design and the implementation in parallel. The central aim is to implement the story with the simplest possible solution. At the end of a story implementation you should have designed, realized in software and unit tested a simple solution.

The documentation of the design should be retrieved as far as possible from the source code. This prevents source code and documentation from running separately and from being inconsistent. The tests of the system are carried out at the level of the software components (unit tests, see Section 2.5) and at the level of acceptance tests, as provided by the users.

The qualifications for a programmer in an XP project include:

- Knowledge of all technologies used in the project (programming languages, database, application server, Web server, etc.)[1]

- Good communication skills

- Good conflict management skills (not only the ability to express criticism appropriately, but also constructive use of criticism)

3.3 Tester

In XP, unit tests (see Section 2.5) are so strongly interwoven into programming that programmers always carry out the unit tests themselves. Therefore, the tester focuses on the acceptance tests that are relevant for the user. The tester helps the users formulate the acceptance tests and implement them with suitable test tools.

---

1. This is a goal in an XP project. One developer will master a particular technology or a chosen topic area better than another developer. By programming in pairs, this inequality of ability and knowledge is balanced out in time, so that ultimately all programmers have mastered all the technologies that are used.

Regardless of whether the acceptance tests are supported by tools, the tester is responsible for carrying out the acceptance tests regularly. This gives the tester an insight into the progress of the project, which is agreed with the 'tracker' (see Section 3.4).

Testers need to have a good insight into the application domain and the developed system in order to be able to carry out tests meaningfully. If they do not have this, the testers will concentrate on minor details (such as fonts and alignment of text fields) and lose sight of the overall functionality.

If the role of the tester is assigned to a single person who has testing as a main responsibility, programming and testing is separated and problems commonly occur. In XP projects, the tester role is taken on by the programmers. This may seem unusual: the literature always postulates that developers should not test their own code. However, although testing is carried out by the programmers, each programmer may test all the code and not just their own. The Test-First principle removes the differentiation between programmers and testers.

3.4 Tracker

The tracker is the 'conscience' of the team. He observes the development process and points out possible problems. To do this, the tracker collects information during the development process, by talking to the developers and collecting quantitative data.

The tracker is responsible for the collection and processing of project data. In XP projects, the data collected is sparse but specific. The tracker should follow the guideline 'Do not collect data if you do not know what you want to do with it'. Typically, the following data is collected (see also [Jeffries *et al.* 00]):

- Project budget

- Total actual cost

- Total actual cost of this iteration

- Expected cost of the next iteration

- Project progress

- Estimated cost of this iteration (from the story cards)

- Outstanding costs in this iteration (in accordance with the estimations of the story cards)

- Velocity of the project team (that is, the ratio of programming time to the total working time)[2]

The data collected by the tracker can be used to control the project further. It helps the project to keep focused and provides useful information for estimating in the next planning game, since the Yesterday's Weather principle [Beck and Fowler 00] is based upon the numbers of the former iterations.

On the basis of this data, the project team can decide how the process should be changed. For example, the project team can establish, using the ratio of the cost that has been accumulated in the current iteration to the remaining cost and the remaining time, that the project has fallen behind schedule. A typical reaction to delay in a project is to reduce the functionality. The developers would therefore hold a discussion with the customer about possible reductions in functionality.

The tracker not only has the task of collecting and processing data. He also independently selects the data that should be collected during the current state of the project. It rarely makes sense to collect the same data over the entire course of the project and to provide the same statistics all the time.

Example   One of our projects had a very high load factor. We addressed this by developing in 'sprints'. Sprints reduce the load factor by removing any tasks that do not further the project (see Section 5.4). After a few sprints, the load factor oscillated in a range between 1.0 and 1.2 and we stopped focusing on it. The information had become useless: we could not improve any more at this point. The tracker was responsible for noticing this and adjusting the collection of data. However, the tracker was also responsible for keeping an eye on the load factor and starting to collect the data again if he thought that it was increasing again.

3.5 XP Coach

XP looks simple. But it is not easy to start with XP successfully without any experience. There are a number of reasons for this. A good part of the learning of XP depends on the discipline of the developer. If the necessary discipline is lacking, the XP development process can fall apart during the learning phase. The dependencies between the XP practices can impact negatively on each other: if, for example, no more unit tests are written, refactoring becomes impossible; if no more refactorings are carried out,

---

2. The velocity is not however the only measure of the effectiveness of a development team. Compare the discussion of load factor in Section 2.2.

simple design can lead to big problems. In contrast to the learning phase, the use of XP practices in an experienced team requires only a little discipline. The XP values and practices become so much second nature to the developers that the XP process just happens.

However, it is advisable to have an XP coach in a new XP project. This coach is responsible for answering questions asked by the team, for finding a suitable introductory strategy and for investigating the ongoing XP development process in order to identify possible problems. In our view, it makes sense that the XP coach should be experienced and should have already contributed to XP projects.

Successful XP projects are still relatively few and far between. Adequately qualified XP coaches are therefore not always easy to find. In this case, the XP coach can be recruited from the project. He should support the XP ideas and acquire as much XP knowledge as he can. An adequate learning phase for the coach then has to be taken into account.

If an experienced XP coach is available, then the project should use this support. The use of a coach is a great deal cheaper and less risky than independent learning. Ways in which XP can be introduced and learnt are described in more detail in Chapter 6.

3.6 Consultant

The consultant advises the project team in technologies that the team has not yet mastered. In order to reduce the truck factor, the consultant is not simply called into the project in order to solve a problem. Instead, the team tries to integrate the necessary special knowledge into the project for the long-run.

The project can gain the specialist knowledge in a number of ways. For example, the consultant may give the whole team an introduction to the technology. Then the consultant can work with various programming pairs to solve urgent problems. This greatly reduces the probability that the team requires a consultant for the same technology again.

The role of the consultant is played by different people for different technologies. The consultant may come from another company or from another project in the same company.

This perception of the work of the consultant is different from the usual practice. Frequently, a consultant comes in to solve a problem and then disappears again. In XP, the consultant is more like an instructor. If the XP team requires a consultant, the perception of the consultant has to be taken into account in selecting a suitable person.

3.7 Big Boss

The role of the Big Boss is relatively vague in Kent Beck's description. The Big Boss makes important decisions about the future of the project and supports the project team in its work. Elsewhere, we tend to hear that the Big Boss controls the financial and human resources of the project. It is not however completely clear whether the Big Boss comes from the developer or the user organisation.

We do not, therefore, use the role of the Big Boss. In our model, the customer role makes the essential decisions on the part of the user organisation and provides the financial backing for the project. The project owners make the decisions about the development process.

3.8 Experiences

In many projects, we split the customer role into the role of the client and the role of the user (see the following sections). The client is responsible for setting goals and the central decisions in the projects, whilst the user provides the domain-specific knowledge and makes smaller decisions. In particular, several users may be integrated into the project (e.g. in the case of multi-channel applications[3]). The integration of several customers into a project would be problematic because it would not be clear who makes the final decision.

The splitting of roles into user and client can, of course, add a communication cost. If technical and financial decisions come into conflict with one another, two people or roles have to come to an agreement. If both roles are filled by one person, this saves time during the course of the project. Since XP mandates simple and lightweight solutions, it seems natural to only have one person. However, problems can occur if both roles are filled by one person, who is normally from the user department. The management or financial responsibilities then stand outside the project to a certain extent and are no longer directly integrated into the planning and implementation of the project. Experience shows that this can be problematic so, whenever possible, we split the customer role into user and client.

---

3. In this context, 'multi-channel' means that an application provides different front-ends for different groups of users. For example, in a banking application the customers of the bank may use a Web-based front-end whereas the employees use a highly interactive front-end to work on the instruction the customer submitted via the Web. You can imagine a large number of different front-ends.

Client

The client provides the financial background for the project and defines the goals of the project. As a rule, he defines the goals by taking into account business policy (e.g. reduction in costs in a specific area of 30%). This method of setting goals still leaves room for manoeuvre in the practical design of the system by users and developers.

Since the client defines the business goals of the project, he also checks whether or not these goals are achieved. Whether a project is a success or not depends on the client. To achieve success, the client has to accept a few commitments:

- He has to be available for questions about the business goals.

- He has to create ways of accessing domain-specific knowledge. If the client is a manager in the user organisation, he can allow the developers access to the users.

- He must take part in the planning game for every release (see Section 4.3). He is also the primary recipient of each release.

- He may take part in the planning game for iterations.

The main client may delegate any of these tasks to the user or another representative.

User

In contrast to the client, the user does not focus on the business goals but on the domain-specific knowledge. Questions about the application domain are answered by the user.

In our experience, it is important to differentiate between two areas of domain-specific knowledge: application logic and operational practices. The application logic includes the business processes and the domain-specific logic (such as, calculation rules). You can read about application logic in parts of the domain-related literature (e.g. tax law, payroll accounting). A representative from the lower or middle management of the user organisation is frequently a suitable contact person for the business processes.

Operational practices concern the tasks the user performs at their work station. Work is done not according to the book and supervisors frequently have an idealised picture of how their employees operate. Knowledge of how tasks are handled in practice is indispensable for constructing a truly useful system.

With this knowledge, the user can have a central role in the design of the system. In the context of the business goals defined by the customer, he sets the subordinate goals for the design of the system and states when these should be attained.

The user writes the story cards, either alone or with the programmers, that define the requirements of the system. He also defines – if necessary, in cooperation with the programmer – the acceptance tests for each function of the system. On the basis of the acceptance tests, the user tests new versions of the system.

The qualifications of a user in an XP project include the following:

- He has to know the application domain. He should not only know the domain-specific logic but should have an accurate idea of the tasks and how they are carried out.

- The user should be receptive to new technologies, otherwise there is the danger that the user simply transfers the concepts of existing systems to the new system. In the worst case, this results in a host application hidden behind graphical window elements.

- The user should have his own incentive for taking part in the project. He should expect personal gain from his cooperation (e.g. a salary increase or promotion, but even the promise of better software support in the future can be a strong motivation) or should expect to have fun designing the system. If the user is forced into the project against his will, he will probably not be of much use.

Project manager

The project manager is not given as a role in XP. This is due to the fact that an XP team has its own authority and should make its own decisions about further actions. Many typical tasks of a project manager are taken on by the tracker and others are taken on by the team as a whole.

However, there are a number of tasks that the project team as a whole cannot carry out adequately, for example, the whole area of human resources planning. For this reason, our projects always have a project manager who is not the 'manager' of the project in a traditional sense but is responsible across the whole project. For example, the project manager keeps an overview of which developers are available at what stage in the project. As well as this, he is the primary contact for his supervisors and customers in non-technical matters (such as, the financial aspects of the project).

3.9 Recommendations

- Determine whether you can manage with a simple customer role in the project. If so, do not separate the client and the user. If you require this separation, make it explicit.

- If, during the course of the project, you establish that there is political infighting, check whether splitting the customer role into client and user can rectify the situation.

- Do not neglect the tracker role.

- Think about whether you need a project manager. If you define a project manager, make sure that he does not 'dominate' anything in the project. He is a moderator within the team and a mediator with the world outside the team.

3.10 Literature

Beck, Kent. 2000. *Extreme Programming Explained: Embrace Change.* Reading, Massachusetts, Addison-Wesley.
  Original description of the roles in XP.

Beck, Kent, and Fowler, Martin. 2000. *Planning Extreme Programming.* Reading, Massachusetts, Addison-Wesley.
  This book gives a detailed insight into the planning of XP projects.

Jeffries, Ron, Anderson, Ann, and Hendrickson, Chet. 2000. *Extreme Programming Installed.* Reading, Massachusetts, Addison-Wesley.
  The members of the C3 project team give the reader a number of hints and tips, including a discussion of the project data that is useful to collect.

4

Artefacts

People reify recurring actions and routines into artefacts. So, the hammer reifies the action of putting a nail into a piece of wood and a bowl reifies the action of storing a liquid. The concept of artefacts can also be found consistently in the area of software development. Version control systems reify the versioning of source texts as well as certain cooperation models (pessimistic vs. optimistic model). Project plans support the planning process and class diagrams can give an overview of an object-oriented system.

In this chapter, we describe the artefacts that are relevant to XP projects (story cards, task cards, release plan, iteration plan). In the process we see the artefacts as a collection of tools that we use when we need them. Since artefacts are primarily characterised by how they are used, we concentrate on describing what they are used for in the development process.

In this chapter, we begin with the description of each artefact and introduce possible adaptations. With the help of the adaptations, aspects of the original XP artefacts can be more strongly emphasised.

4.1 Story cards

Index cards Story cards can have completely different forms. In our projects, we use A5 index cards. The physical presence of index cards can have a number of advantages. Therefore, index cards should be written freely and notes for which records need to be kept are jotted down directly onto the cards. If a card is complete, the developers put it in the 'complete' pile, which gives them a liberating and satisfying feeling. Some developers go to the pile of complete story cards every day to get a 'concrete' impression of the progress of the project.

The index cards greatly aid cooperation as well. They guarantee that two pairs of developers are not processing the same cards at the same time.

With a few small annotations on the cards, they can even support processes based on the division of labour. Therefore, a development pair can, for example, start with one card and implement part of the requirement. They integrate their changes and note down the progress on the card. After this, they put the card back on the pile of outstanding cards. The next pair of developers can then work further on this card.

Another important question concerns the assignment of employees to story cards. We prefer to assign cards on a 'first come, first served' basis: the story cards are put into a pile of scheduled cards according to their priority; when a development pair requires work, they take the next card from the pile and process it. The advantage of this practice is its simplicity. The only thing that has to be determined is which story cards are processed and in which order. The rest then takes care of itself. Of course, this practice only works if the developers are equally qualified so that any developer can take care of any task. If this is not the case, we do not change our planning, but bring the developers up to the required level. During a transitional period, explicit assignment of developers to story cards may be necessary. In these cases, we use reference lines to carry out the assignment.

Size of story   Our story cards have a size of one to five pair days. This appears to be a suitable compromise between planning cost and the accuracy of the estimate. Cards with clearly higher costs lead to considerable inaccuracies in estimates. Cards that are a lot smaller make the planning game more difficult because too many story cards have to be dealt with. We have already described the process of estimation in Section 2.2.

Adaptation: Scenarios

XP understands software development primarily as a learning process and recognises that: 'we cannot develop faster than we learn'. However, XP does not make any statements about how the learning process should be meaningfully constructed.

For the last ten years, we have been using accurately defined mechanisms to determine requirements. We carry out interviews with the customers and users. On the basis of these interviews, developers write 'scenarios' that refer to aspects of the user's workplace.

These scenarios have a number of uses. Taking notes helps the developers to clarify what they have heard in the interview. The users can examine the written requirements, thus carrying out an initial validation of the developers' understanding of the application domain. Last but not least, scenarios are an important instrument for spreading knowledge of the application domain amongst the developers. Scenarios do not formalise the application context, but are used as examples. It is more important that the scenarios are easy to read and understand than that they are complete.

Interviews and scenarios are connected to the writing of story cards. Even if developers have only just acquired an initial understanding of the application, they can understand, estimate, and implement story cards. As understanding of the application domain increases, the scenarios are consulted less and less. Frequently, the main function of scenarios is to ensure that, when writing, developers understand how users work.

Whether or not scenarios are necessary depends strongly on the project context. If the team works together closely, shares a common background of experience, and has constant access to users, the explicit writing of scenarios can be done away with.

Scenarios are, however, valuable if the developers have no access to the application domain, if the developers do not have common background experience, or if the project is distributed and is being worked on in different locations.

Example An example scenario could be: 'The consultant picks up his consulting folder, looks for the product in a log, and opens the folder at the appropriate place. The consulting folder also contains a form folder of standard forms (such as third-party contracts) and a sample folder with guides for filling in contract and master document forms.'

Business use cases Scenarios are similar to UML business use cases. Both describe an existing situation and do not look at the future system; they are used to understand the existing work tasks. Scenarios and business use cases differ from UML use cases. Use cases are targeted at the system to be developed and thus to the future.

Adaptation: Glossary

An important building block for the learning process in the development project is the presence of shared concepts between developers and users. Only if all those taking part use a common vocabulary can requirements be formulated precisely.

The glossary reifies the shared concepts. Developers record important terms in the glossary. The glossary contains terms specific to the application domain (for example, the term 'cover' in the field of insurance) and relevant technological terms (for example, window, mouse, double-click), for the benefit of the user. The terms in the glossary are oriented primarily to the technical language of the user.

The glossary is central to the establishment of a common and clear-cut project language. It can be extremely obstructive to the development of a software system if several terms are used to express the same or similar concepts.

Table 4.1 Sample glossary entry

Product	A product defines the *proposal* of an *insurance company* to *prospective customers*. The product determines which preconditions are valid for the agreement of a *contract* and which *payments* are provided by the insurance company in the case of a *claim*. The name of the product is an important component of every *insurance contract*.

Index cards

For example, in an insurance project, the terms 'object' and 'risk' were used almost synonymously, which gave rise to confusion about the terms. At the first attempt, the developers could not agree on how to name the respective classes and this unclear concept also lead to confusion concerning the responsibilities of the implemented classes.

Maintaining the glossary

A glossary can be used in a similar way to scenarios to consolidate the developers' technical understanding. In this case, it plays a large part during the early stages of the project and becomes less important as the project goes on. Alternatively, the glossary can be used as a dictionary for the project. Newcomers can use it to become familiar with the project more easily. Frequently, the glossary is also a suitable underpinning for the user documentation. In this case, the question is who maintains the glossary. Since the glossary is initially written by developers, they also normally maintain it. At first, it may seem natural to let the users maintain the glossary. However, there is the danger that the glossary becomes incomprehensible for the developers and thus useless.

Adaptation: Project diary

The project diary helps make the project easy to understand. Even during the project itself, it can be useful to look back at what has been done. Developers who come back from holiday or from training can quickly get an impression of how far the project has progressed. This is also true for team members who may not work on the project for five days a week.

All team members document the course of the project in the project diary. For this reason, it is sensible to make the project diary available in electronic form (e.g. as a Word document or HTML page).

Content of the diary

The project diary should be as compact as possible and as extensive as necessary. It should not simply be a record of the individual activities of the employees, therefore. It should also record the following types of information:

- Results of investigations, e.g. 'How do I repair a corrupt Visual Age repository?'

- Project progress, e.g. 'Is an initial correct rate for life assurance calculated?'

- Outstanding problems, e.g. 'The EJBs cannot be deployed.'

- Solved problems, e.g. 'The EJBs can be deployed if the most recent service pack of the application server is installed.'

- Instructions from the supervisor, e.g. 'Use the Oracle database!'

- Decisions from customers, e.g. 'We do not need the *foo* function until much later.'

A project diary does not have to be used in every project. The effort needed to maintain it must be weighed up against its expected use. After all, a certain amount of logging is provided by the archived story and task cards. Furthermore, the e-mail traffic between the members of the project can be seen as a kind of project diary. However, e-mail is difficult to read sequentially.

4.2   Task cards

There are technical tasks that are not related to a story card. This relates to technical requirements that do not affect the customer directly. For example, a particularly large refactoring may be important for the development. If you were to write this requirement on a story card and use it in the planning game, the customer would tend to give it a low priority.

Therefore we write such technical requirements on task cards, which are not used in the planning game. They are included in a second round of planning, without the customer, in which we try to assign the task cards to story cards. This makes sure that the relevant task cards are implemented in this iteration and prevents the project from 'playing brilliantly but losing'. This can be a danger if, in the search for the perfect system, the developers carry out refactorings but no longer implement technical requirements.

Index cards   A5 index cards can be used well as task cards. The task cards should however be clearly distinguishable from the story cards, for example, by using a different colour. Task cards can be written on the basis of story cards or on the basis of technical requirements. Task cards are, for example, written by developers who identify a refactoring requirement that they cannot implement straight away. Whether or not story cards are broken down into task cards depends on the project. We have rarely found this to be necessary; more often, we break story cards down into smaller story cards in order to let several pairs work on one story card. We assign developers to task cards in the same way as for the story cards.

Task cards breaking down story cards   Appraisals can be made either on the basis of the story or the task cards. In our projects, we appraise the story cards and let the task cards run unappraised. In our experience, this does not cause any problems.

Size of task   As a rule, task cards are smaller than story cards. In our case, they normally have a maximum cost of two pair days. If the task cards are a lot bigger, it becomes difficult to have them running in an iteration and their immediate benefit cannot be seen as the time taken to implement the task cards would delay the total iteration. If a task card of four person days is assigned to a story card that also has an estimated cost of four days, it cannot really be argued that the task card accelerates the implementation of the story card.

Consider this example from an insurance company project.

Example

Story Card 1
The employee is looking for a customer in the host portfolio. The search can be carried out according to first name, surname, customer number, existing contract number, street, postal code, city.
Estimate: four jelly babies.

Since the story card is relatively large, several pairs should work on this in parallel. We could break the card down according to different criteria. A technical breakdown into task cards may look as follows:
Task Card 1 for Story Card 1
Extend the class `CustomerManager` so that customers can be found according to the criteria mentioned.

Task Card 2 for Story Card 1
Develop the user interface for the customer finder.

Task Card 3 for Story Card 1
Develop the customer finder with access to the user interface from task card 2 and the customer manager from task card 1.

Alternatively, you could break the above story card down into smaller story cards.

Story Card 1a
The employee is looking for a customer in the host portfolio. The search is carried out according to the customer number.

Story Card 1b
The search for the customer can be carried out via street, postal code, city.

Story Card 1c
The search for the customer can be carried out via the contract number.

The second breakdown has the advantage that it can be discussed with the customer, who can even influence its priority. However, the first breakdown is probably more suitable for parallel work because you can develop task cards 1 and 2 completely independently from one another. In the second breakdown, you would have to merge the individual results but this is not normally too dramatic. After all, we invest most of the time in learning and not in typing. In addition, story card 1c can be developed independently from cards 1a and 1b because the search is carried out in another portfolio (contract data).

The main problem with this story is that, in both of the breakdowns, the first card (task card 1 or story card 1a) are much more costly than the other two cards: the mainframe system has to be accessed for the first time there. The team could try to break down task card 1 even further or look at the documentation for gateway products which allow access to the mainframe system. If the team does not want to incur the risk caused by this unknown factor in their estimation, they can create a Spike Solution for the mainframe access. This works equally well with both breakdowns.

Virtual task cards are often created when developers are processing story cards. Let's assume that we have broken down story card 1 according to the second strategy. A pair takes card 1a and starts to implement it. They briefly think about how the requirement can be implemented and establish that a CICS connection may be suitable. They must identify the CICS program to be called and check whether it meets the requirements. The pair writes these single steps either on the back of the story card or on task cards that are stapled to the story card. If the story card is to be developed in parallel, the task cards can be allocated to other pairs.

4.3 Release plan

XP tries not to plan too far ahead. Frequently, it only defines the deadline and functions for the next release. The release definition is typically a simple text or a short presentation. As a rule, a detailed plan using, for example, MS Project, is neither necessary nor useful.

In long-running projects, the typical release plan may not be enough. Various parties want the certainty that the total project can be realised in the time frame envisaged. This can be achieved by a staged release plan that contains all releases.

Adaptation: Staged release plan

Large systems cannot be implemented in one release. XP reflects this through its small releases. In many project contexts, we do however require a general overview of the whole system to be developed. This kind of overview is necessary, for example, if a complete host system is to be replaced. In such a project context, the sponsors want an overview of the anticipated stages in the project.

The concept of the staged release plan addresses this problem by defining the releases of the project. Each stage lasts from one to three months.

Backwards planning
The releases are planned backwards – starting from the overall goal and the final deadline, which may be more or less fixed (as in the case of the Year 2000 problem and the conversion to the Euro). Each release has a sub-goal, is implemented in a specific way, and has a target deadline. The result of any release must be able to be appraised by customers and users. The first release may produce a prototype while subsequent releases produce subsystems that can be implemented.

Release plans do not contradict the planning game. Instead, release plans address the need in large projects to create a rough plan that covers a long time span as well as an iteration plan.

Release planning games
The release plan is implemented in special planning games that establish the main emphasis of the next stage. The normal planning games are carried out within the framework of the release plan. The participants may be different in the two types of planning game. The overall release plan can be created by the sponsor and project management, whilst the planning game for the iterations is carried out by developers and users. As a rule, other people also take part in the planning game for the release plan. Frequently, development team and user representatives are involved.

Table 4.2 Example release plan

Sub-goal	Implementation	When
Executive board accepts reorganisation concept.	Demo: Administration prototype plus account management scenarios, glossary, and visions (scenarios for the future)	31 March
Central development reduces architecture.	Review: Laboratory prototype with connection to host computer and relational database.	16 May

Sub-goal	Implementation	When
Executive board accepts reorganised core process.	Demo: Pilot account manager workstation in a branch office of a bank.	30 September
Executive board is convinced by feasibility of the concept.	Report: Account manager workstation in three banks in the company.	1 December
Revision certifies system.	Review: Software documented and tested in accordance with the project handbook.	10 December
Executive board accepts first release.	Workshop with users.	15 February

Adaptation: Core system with special systems

XP's small releases lead to sequential procedures. Since the number of developers in an XP team cannot be increased arbitrarily, the maximum speed of development is limited. If, for example, a complete legacy system is replaced, the project can last for a long time.

XP projects work with a maximum of 20 developers. In order to reduce the length of a very large development project, it can be divided into several XP projects. This however poses a question of the criteria by which the individual XP projects are formed and how they are synchronised.

These problems are addressed by developing the concept of a core system, which implements the important core functions of the system, surrounded by special systems that implement additional functions. The special systems are supported by the core system but do not depend on each other. Because of this, it is possible to begin developing the special systems as soon as the first version of the core system is complete. The special systems can then be released in any sequence or in parallel, with several project teams.

Example   A hospital project defined a core system with special systems (see [Krabbel *et al.* 96a]). Patient administration, admissions, transfer of patients, etc. were identified as the core system (see Figure 4.1). The systems for the support of operations (OP system), for archiving etc. were declared as special systems. This established that the functions of the core system satisfied the most urgent requirements and also that the special systems could not work without the functions of the core system.

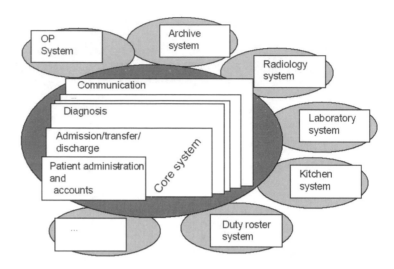

Figure 4.1 Core system and special systems

If the special systems are used to run several XP projects in parallel, the development process is less flexible. If the division between special systems is fundamentally changed, the XP projects may have to be organised differently. For example, if two special systems are consolidated, the XP projects also have to be consolidated. Such changes to the organisational structure are relatively time-consuming, as a rule, because the developers will need to get used to working in a new project.

However, this reduction of flexibility is not due to the special systems. It always occurs if several XP projects have to be synchronised. If the parts of the system assigned to the individual projects are evaluated differently, both the organisation and the cooperation of the projects are affected.

4.4 Iteration plan

A release consists of several iterations. Iterations are planned through the assignment and prioritisation of story and task cards. Sometimes it can be helpful to detail this planning further using base lines.

Adaptation: Base lines

Young and inexperienced XP project members sometimes have problems with the free contact with story and task cards. In this case, it makes sense to have a transitional period in which the team explicitly plans in advance who is responsible for which tasks.

Base lines can be used for the detailed planning within releases. Unlike release plans, base lines do not fix a date for their completion. For every task it is specified who is responsible for it, what is to be done, why it is to be done, and how the handling is checked. In particular, the point of the action is often surprising. Sometimes software developers think that they have to do something, but they do not really know why. This may be an indication that the task is superfluous. Superfluous tasks cannot happen in an XP project that has been carried out correctly. Because story cards are only created by customers or users, it is guaranteed that the individual requirements are justified. If the project team is still inexperienced with XP, 'pseudo-requirements' may appear. Base lines can uncover pseudo-requirements that only the developers believe are necessary.

Table 4.3 Example base lines

Who	Do what with whom/what	What for	How it is checked
PB	Arrange deadline arrangements with pilot bank.	Preparing interviews.	E-mail to the team.
RS	Work out interview guidelines.	Preparing interviews.	Presentation at the meeting.
PB, RS, DM	Interview account managers.	Giving basis for scenarios.	Protocols in the DB project.
DM	Create tool framework.	Preparing tool implementation.	Operational laboratory prototype of tool.
AK, WS	Design and implement a contract tool.	Testing framework; preparing user workshop.	Operational laboratory prototype of tool.

Base lines are a tabular representation of story and task cards and should not be necessary. However, if the project has still not reached the XP ideal state, base lines can give the members of the project valuable assistance in organising their work. In particular, if the technical abilities and knowledge in the team are still unequal, the explicit assignment of tasks to individual members of the project can be necessary. It must however be clear that the assignment of tasks to individual development pairs is always a provisional solution. There should be a vigorous attempt to get all developers so well qualified that the explicit allocation of tasks is no longer necessary. Base lines can act as 'stabilizers' (learning aids) during the introduction of XP. The project has to learn to get by without stabilizers as quickly as possible.

4.5 Literature

Krabbel, A., Ratuski, S., and Wetzel, I. 1996a. 'Requirements Analysis of Joint Tasks in Hospitals' in *Proceedings of IRIS* 19(2):10–13. Gothenburg Studies in Informatics, Lökeberg, Sweden.
This article describes a core system and its construction stages.

Lilienthal, C., and Züllighoven, H. 1997. 'Application-Oriented Use Quality: The tools and materials approach' in *Interactions Magazine*, IV(6), ACM.
This articlediscusses how interviews, scenarios and glossaries contribute to the creation of high-quality software.

Organisation

5

5.1 Defining requirements

Defining the requirements of the system to be developed is critical for every software project. The general aim of defining requirements is that developers and users agree on which functionality the future system should realise and in which way. XP understands the definition of requirements as a general learning process for the users and developers. The developers learn which tasks the users perform and how they take care of these tasks. The users learn the possibilities for support through modern hardware and software systems.

These days, more and more customers understand that a final definition of requirements at the start of the project is usually impossible. From the outset, a cyclical development process is recommended. Thus, functionality can be implemented and used even before all details of the future sub-systems are finally fixed. We define requirements throughout a project, but we give the developers an introduction to the topic and the domain-specific knowledge at the start. The practices of 'open interviews' and, occasionally, workplace observations are valuable at this stage.

Open interviews
In open interviews, the developers question the users about their work in one-to-one conversations. Open interviews are based on open questions that cannot be answered by simple facts or one-word answers. The developers ask their questions frankly so that the users are encouraged to answer them freely. This gives the user control over the sequence of the interview and the weight given to each topic. The user's focus in the interview often gives important hints for the main focus of the system development. As a rule, the user will talk in detail about the topic that plays an important role in his or her daily work. On the other hand, the interviewer must also steer the interview in the right direction. The users may want to talk about issues that are not relevant to the development.

In our experience, it is better to interview people one at a time. As a rule, it is more pleasant for the user. It is also important to choose carefully the user to be questioned. The groups of intended users must be identified relatively early on in the development process, to enable the developers to identify suitable interview partners. The head of the department and other managers usually want to be interviewed, but they are often too far removed from the daily routine to give the developers the necessary information. They may not use the application system at all or only in a very limited way. In particular, they tend to talk about idealised procedures that have not been put into practice in the organisation. However, it makes sense on both a practical and a political level to interview the managers, as they will influence the aims and objectives of the development.

Once interview partners have been selected, the developers then carry out one or more interviews with at least one representative from each user group/role. This is necessary because users in different roles, quite rightly, usually have a completely different perspective on the processes and developers run the risk of missing out on important aspects because they have spoken to the wrong or too few users.

Even if all these points are taken into account, unfortunately there is no safe and simple way to validate the requirements definition. It is always possible that the developers have spoken to the "wrong" users or that the important user roles were not identified. In any event, the validation of the requirements definition ultimately takes place when the system is being used. This is another reason why it is so important to start implementing usable parts of the system as soon as possible.

Whilst we recommend that only one user is questioned at a time, it is a good idea to have two people interviewing. As a rule, it is too much to ask that a single person provides the structure for the interview and also takes the minutes. We therefore recommend that one developer carries out the interview and another developer takes the minutes. The two developers can then sit together and clear up any uncertainties. They can make notes (e.g. a record of the interview, scenarios, a glossary), which can be used as the basis for feedback with the users. The feedback session is a vehicle for further investigating the domain-specific knowledge of the user and outstanding questions can be cleared up.

Workplace observations The interviews are best carried out at the user's workplace. Objectivity is very important when learning the requirements. We can remember correlations much more easily if we can see how objects are used (e.g. an application form in an insurance company, follow-up files of a bank, resuscitation equipment in a hospital). If the users are at their workplaces, they will have such objects to hand as aids for explanation. If, on the other hand, the interviews are carried out in the room where the developers work, or in a meeting room, this back tracking is made more difficult. If the interview cannot be located in a place where the users work, then they should at least be asked to bring some example objects to the interview. Alternatively, workplace observations can be carried out at a different time from the interviews.

Scenarios As well as seeing how the objects are used, workplace observations allow a direct impression to be obtained from the work context of the user. It is often overlooked that the situation at the workplace is an important factor in designing the system. For example, a system that uses modal dialogue boxes is not suitable in an environment in which the users are often interrupted by telephone calls whose replies require the system. Workplace observations also enable developers to see directly how and with which objects the users deal.

This approach may seem unnecessary if the users are already working with software systems, but amazing discoveries can be made in these situations: occasionally, lists are made by hand, items on a printout are ticked, or information is copied laboriously from one form into another. In short: at the user's workplace, the developer can learn a lot about the requirements of the future system.

We regard scenarios, also called business use cases in the UML framework, as suitable documents for obtaining feedback from the users about the domain concepts that have been understood by the developers. These documents do not replace direct conversation with the users, but can be used as a starting point for the discussion. Scenarios document functional requirements and a generic exemplary description of the task. In creating scenarios, the developers first start with the IS status, which clarifies and describes the business rules that apply. In later steps, one can approach the desired SHALL status and discuss changes to the existing process.

Glossary   Many of the users' technical terms are used in the scenarios. Developers keep their understanding of these terms in a glossary, on which the user also gives feedback. The glossary represents an important concept model, and many of the terms described appear later in the design of the software system.

XP practices   There is a strong link between requirements definition and the planning game (see Section 2.2). You can obtain good feedback about the system to be created from the on-site customer (see Section 2.1), in the context of small releases (see Section 2.4).

In many ways, our experiences and practices are similar to the approaches described in [Rising 00]. We see requirements definition not as a phase but as an activity. Whilst a phase has start and end points and a result, activities are carried out over and over again and modify existing results. This perspective is in tune with XP: we only define requirements as we need them.

Example   A customer would like a system which puts business processes onto the Web. Neither he nor the developers are clear about how this can actually be done. With the available knowledge on both parts, no meaningful story cards can be written. The developers start to talk to users and developers who have worked in similar areas before. The results of the interviews are noted in scenarios and are discussed with the customers. During this discussion, the developers and users build up a general idea about the future system and initial story cards can be written. The story cards are then stored and implemented. As soon as the developers start asking questions that the customer cannot answer, new interviews are carried out and new scenarios are written.

5.2   Project planning

The planning of software development projects is anything but easy. The estimation of the required programming cost and the specification of a completion date is difficult, even if there is a precise and complete requirements specification. In the previous section, however, we have set the bar even higher and want to proceed in a cyclical manner without detailed requirements.

Even if the cyclical procedure appears to be contrary to a development plan, it does not only apply to the advance planning of the project. If the planning is cyclical and regularly revised, with estimations carried out on the basis of experiences from previous cycles, then there is a higher probability that the plan will act as a safety-net: it will be more realistic. This experience is also described in [Jeffries *et al.* 2000].

Target group:
clients

For whom is project planning carried out, predominantly? And how relevant it is to different groups? The ordering customer (the client) is not interested in the details of the project planning. He is mainly interested in whether the project is being carried out in the planned financial and time frameworks. In this context, the client wants to be convinced, in general terms, that the project is going according to plan.

Target group:
users

The users are interested in whether individual story cards are handled in the desired sequence. They are not interested in which developer works on which story card. The business goals of the client are also relevant to the users. If the users are unclear about the goals of the client, they have difficulties prioritising story cards appropriately.

The division of the customer role into clients and users can cause a conflict. The two roles usually have different perspectives of the project and may even have diverging goals. This conflict then has to be dealt with in the project.

Target group: developers

Programmers are interested in both the business goals of the client and the story cards. Achievement of the objectives and implementation of the story cards are the primary criteria for the success of the development project. The programmers also plan a number of technical aspects, including large refactorings, the use of application servers, or a new database. A feature of XP projects is that the domain aspects always have priority and technologies are always understood as a means to an end. XP projects try to couple technical tasks to requirements during the planning stage to reduce the danger that time is spent unnecessarily on technologies. The project team is also responsible for the resource planning in the project. The members of the project must, for example, coordinate their holiday plans with each other.

This means that planning is under no circumstances carried out by users alone. In fact, users, developers, and their respective management all take part in the planning. The developers clarify which resources are available for the next version and estimate the cost for individual story cards, while the users prioritise the cards in a planning game.

In principle, we base project planning on the artefacts: story and task cards, release plans and, if necessary, base lines.

5.3 Contract formation

Conventional contract models

Conventional software development contracts are processed as either fixed-price or cost-dependent projects. In the fixed-price model, the development organisation estimates the total cost of the project, based on a requirements definition that is as complete as possible. This requirements definition is created by the customers or a third party (e.g. a management consultant). If the project is cost-dependent, the development organisation makes monthly calculations about the money that has been used up on the basis of previously negotiated hourly or daily rates.

Software development projects always carry risks. In fixed-price projects, the customer appears to have security concerning these risks. If the software is not delivered or is not of adequate quality, the customer can refuse to pay or reduce the amount. However, this security is misleading. The experiences of the last decade of software development clearly show that requirements for non-trivial software systems cannot be completely and explicitly formulated. Furthermore, the requirements only become clear during the project, or change during the course of the project. Therefore, unsuccessful development projects end up in court. If this happens, both the customer and the development organisation are the losers: the development organisation only gets part of the agreed amount and loses a customer. Even if the development organisation does not have to pay for the failure, it has wasted a lot of time and effort and has to redraft the whole development project.

Cyclical projects   At first glance, cyclical projects seem to be incompatible with fixed-price projects: the total extent of the cost cannot be estimated before the start of the project. In fact, such projects make explicit the facts that are true of every software development project. It is obvious that traditional fixed-price projects are only suitable for a few software development projects. XP projects have successfully used various contract models.

Budget basis   If the contract works on a budget basis, the customer states the objective and makes a budget available for the project. If necessary, a prototype is created with a sub-budget.

Fixed price after   If the customer insists on a fixed-price contract, it can be agreed after a
pre-project   pre-project. In the pre-project, the developers clarify the technical requirements and create prototypes. This guarantees that, after the pre-project, the customer can assign the project to a development organisation. The cost of the pre-project can be settled according to how much money has been used or according to the fixed price. This method also has its limitations: projects of more than 200 person days contain a certain estimation risk and projects with more than 400 person days are almost impossible to estimate after a pre-project.

Costs and   XP projects can also use a contract that mixes fixed-price and cost-
premium   dependent terms. During the development, the customer pays the developer's salary every month. When a component is delivered, a premium is paid. The extent of this depends on whether it is delivered before time, at the right time, or late.

All XP projects aim for the frequent delivery of usable system components. This method significantly reduces the project risks. Even if the project is interrupted, the customer still has the parts of the system that have already been developed.

5.4 Sprints

Sprints (see [Beedle *et al.* 00]) are short periods, up to a maximum of three weeks, during which the developers of a team focus as much as possible on the development of the software system. This may sound odd, since the developers have their whole work time dedicated to the project and they usually work in a focused way. However, it is often not the case that they are wholly focused for 100% of the time, which has less to do with the developers themselves than the organisations in which they work. Even developers who are assigned to the project full time have holidays, go on training courses, visit further education institutions, participate in maintenance tasks and error corrections in pre-projects, etc.

If a project requires it, sprints can help as they define a fixed time period during which there can be no disruptions from outside the project. The distractions, or 'troublemakers', can be allocated time after the sprint. The main troublemaker is always the telephone. In our experience, the project manager should not take part in the sprint but should take over the role of telephonist in order to prevent his development team from being disrupted. Sometimes, the developer cannot obtain the necessary protection in his normal workplace. It is then necessary that the whole team looks for another place to work, e.g. a hotel, a seminar room, or another branch office of the company.

During a sprint, the density of work and the concentration of the individual developers may be a lot higher over a considerably longer period of time than most developers are used to. Programming in pairs is exhausting anyway, but the reduction of external sources of interference increases the density even further. Therefore, we do not sprint for weeks at a time and we make a conscious effort to take breaks more frequently. As well as providing relaxation, the breaks also provide time for the developers to talk about the development, including the designs and implementations of the project. This reflection on their own work is necessary and very helpful for the project.

We have been developing the JWAM framework for about two years in sprints lasting three days persss month, because it does not have a dedicated development team. One of our recommendations for successful sprints is that, if possible, the team should remain constant throughout the sprint. New developers added to the project always have to be brought up to date, which can clearly reduce the speed of the development.

We always give sprints a social dimension and, towards the end of the sprint, organise a sprint party. This can be a meal, a game of cricket, or some other activity. Sprint parties are understood by the developers as a small thank you for their commitment. If at all possible, the costs for the sprint party should be met by the employer.

5.5 Stand-up meetings

We have already clearly stressed at several points in this book that communication between developers is good and necessary. Programming in (changing) pairs substantially promotes communication within the development team. But communication is necessary amongst the whole team. Weekly project meetings are often set up for this purpose. However, these meetings can escalate and they often discuss individual issues that are irrelevant to, and therefore boring for, most participants.

The solution to this problem is to hold stand-up meetings (see [Beedle *et al.* 00]) at a fixed time (e.g. before lunch) and have a fixed length, up to 10 to 15 minutes. In order to be able to hold a meeting in such a short time, there are two rules:

- The participants stand up (sometimes people talk about a standing, in contrast to a sitting). It is not a social event where people drink coffee and eat biscuits; there are other shared activities where people can do this. It is a meeting to discuss the progress of the project and to talk about which developers are currently doing what and the problems they are having or the new knowledge that has been gained and is interesting to everybody.

- No discussions are allowed and questions have to be kept short. Anyone wanting to learn more about a topic can sit with the appropriate developers after the meeting and ask them questions. As a rule, such discussions are only interesting to individual members of the project. It is therefore better for the team if the issues are introduced briefly. If necessary, an outcome of the subsequent discussion may be announced in the next meeting. If the topic is relevant to all members of the project, it is advisable to set up a meeting specifically to discuss it. If we do this, the participants have the chance to prepare for this meeting.

5.6 Literature

Beedle, M., *et al.* 2000. 'SCRUM: A Pattern Language for Hyperproductive Software Development' in [Harrison *et al.* 2000], pp. 637–51.
   The concepts of stand-up meetings and sprints are taken from SCRUM.

DeMarco, Tom, and Lister, Timothy. 1999. *Peopleware: Productive Projects and Teams*, second edition. Dorset House.
   This book is a classic on the human factor in software projects.

Harrison, N., Foote, B., and Rohnert, H. (Eds) 2000. *Pattern Languages of Program Design 4*. Reading, Massachusetts, Addison-Wesley.

This book describes SCRUM and further patterns for the formation of development processes. It describes the determination of requirements in cooperative tasks in a hospital project.

Jeffries, Ron, Anderson, Ann, and Hendrickson, Chet. 2000. *Extreme Programming Installed*. Reading, Massachusetts, Addison-Wesley.
The members of the C3 project team explain the concept of XP in detail and give the reader a number of hints and tips along the way.

Krabbel, A., Wetzel, I., and Ratuski, S. 1996c. 'Participation of Heterogeneous User Groups: Providing an Integrated Hospital Information System' in *Proceedings PDC-Conference*, pp. 241–9. Boston.
This paper describes the determination of requirements with different user groups in a hospital project.

Lilienthal, C., and Züllighoven, H. 1997. 'Application-Oriented Use Quality: The tools and materials approach' in *Interactions Magazine*, IV(6), ACM.
This articlediscusses how interviews, scenarios and glossaries can be used in the definition of requirements.

Rising, L. 2000. 'Customer Interaction Patterns' in [Harrison *et al.* 00], pp. 585–609.
This article describes patterns of interaction between users and customers and contains important tips for the definition of requirements.

Implementing XP

6

XP must be learned by doing. The ideas behind XP seem simple and obvious but learning XP is as necessary as it is for other development processes. The question therefore arises as to how the learning process can be arranged for the project team as a whole, as well as for individual members.

As a rule, the members of the project team have already worked with other more or less explicitly formulated development processes. Therefore, it is not just a question of them simply getting to know XP; they also have to unlearn old habits and adapt to new ones. Even if the XP practices are conveyed to the developers, this does not automatically lead to a well-functioning XP development process. The project team has to learn to watch out for symptoms of problems in the development process and to react to these accordingly.

XP is frequently accused of having a 'hacker' mentality, meaning that it is completely unplanned and anarchically organised. It should be quite clear from what we have stated in the previous chapters that this is not the case at all. In fact, the reverse is correct: learning and implementing XP requires quite a lot of discipline from all those involved, not just programmers. If XP is to be used for a project, the correct boundary conditions must also be created in both the management of the project and its organisation.

In this chapter, we give suggestions and tips for how XP can be learnt and implemented in a company. We focus first on the development team. In later sections, we address the question of how the management can deal with an XP process and how the necessary context for an XP project can be created. To conclude, we describe our impression of how XP can be established in companies.

Working on an XP project can be fun for developers. This is good, as fun increases motivation and, in the right amounts, can have positive effects on the project. After all, we all prefer working in a pleasant environment. There are a number of games that help to learn XP and practice the techniques. Since we have had quite good experiences with them, we briefly describe two of these possibilities at the end of the chapter.

6.1 Implementation strategies

The development team is the group of programmers whose task it is to realise the software system. There are a number of schools of thought about how one can bring home the ideas and practices of XP to a development team: you can introduce the complete package through a series of presentations and training exercises or you can gradually introduce individual practices, building up to a complete implementation of XP.

Normally, it isn't a good idea to introduce XP into an existing project as a complete package. A gradual introduction is more suitable as work in the project does not then need to be stopped. This way of introducing XP into an existing project complies with the philosophy of XP: in an XP project we proceed gradually and break up large changes to the system into smaller refactorings that can be carried out in small steps. The advantages of this procedure (high security, no disruptions) can be transferred to the introduction of XP into a working team. The team can carry on working on the system and learn the new practices one step at a time and weave them into the development process.

Sequence for introducing practices

This does, of course, create the question of the order in which single practices can be meaningfully integrated into the team. In general, one cannot define a *correct* sequence for introducing the practices. The sequence that is chosen must suit the context of the project and must be able to be integrated into the daily work. Nevertheless, since not every possible sequence is meaningful, we can give some tips from having introduced the practices gradually into some of our projects.

The technique of unit testing can be introduced independently from the other practices without any problems. This is also true of pair programming, however, appropriate coding conventions should be agreed beforehand, because otherwise pair programming can be extremely difficult and exhausting. Collective ownership makes pair programming easier and makes a big improvement in its own right. Having a general metaphor for the future system is also one of the elementary practices on which others are built. Therefore, the metaphors should be defined as early on as possible. A project can successfully integrate XP practices in the following order:

1. Metaphor, coding conventions, unit tests

2. Collective ownership, pair programming

3. Simple designs, refactoring (these practices do not need any others as preconditions and complement each other well)

4. Continuous integration

5. On-site customer, planning game, acceptance tests, small releases (these practices cannot easily be separated from one another or used without the related practices)

Small releases appear to be independent of the other practices but they play an important part in the planning game. If appropriate feedback is not obtained from the customer about a release, it loses meaning for the development team.

6. Sustainable pace

This technique follows almost automatically. If the development team uses the other practices, there is less and less necessity to work overtime.

The sequence that we have suggested here is only one possible sequence that we have practised successfully. In other contexts, other sequences can be meaningful. They depend on the experience of the developer and the project context.

Solve the biggest problem first Another useful strategy is to introduce first the XP technique that solves the biggest problem in the project. If the biggest problem is the stability of the created software, then one would introduce unit tests first. If the requirements in the project are unclear, the introduction of the on-site user and the planning game is recommended. If the developed system is difficult to maintain, this problem can be remedied by simple design and refactoring.

In an existing project, the gradual introduction of XP can guarantee that the work on the software system is not negatively influenced. The developers are not detached from the development by a two-week training course, but can learn XP during their daily project work and can use the practices they have learnt. By doing this, they quickly gain experience with the practices they have used.

There is of course the danger that not all XP practices are used. For the team, it is a relatively large temptation to use only the immediately beneficial practices and to resist further innovations. In the end, this means that the team has only mastered and used part of the XP practices. The cooperation of all the practices is not practised and the team does not carry out a 'true' XP project. This of course also means that some of the advantages of XP remain unused.

In our experience, one cannot decide which method of introduction is more suitable without knowing the context of the project. We have had quite good experiences with the 'eXtreme Hour' (Section 6.7). On the other hand, we have introduced XP slowly into our framework development and have likewise had good experiences. However, we have also seen that a gradual introduction of XP without an experienced coach can become relatively expensive. The team makes a lot of errors that the trainer has already seen; an XP coach would have spared us many dead-ends.

Our experience has shown that the introductory phase of XP is difficult and problematic. The team needs to be very disciplined. The XP practices can also be practised and learnt in the form of suitable games (the 'eXtreme Hour' and the 'eXplanations Game' are described in Section 6.7).

6.2   The XP coach

However you introduce XP, weaknesses and errors have to be recognised early on so that the team can be steered in the right direction. If errors are only recognised when it is too late in the procedure, they may have already been established and may be very difficult to remove from the team culture. Therefore, we strongly recommend that you consult an experienced XP coach who can accompany the team throughout the learning phase.

In a development project, the XP coach ensures the correct and most effective use of the XP ideas and practices. The XP trainer does not necessarily need previous XP experience, although that would make his job easier. He supports the team. He makes the team aware of problems and helps the team to work out ways of solving them. He identifies weaknesses in the process as early as possible and eliminates them before they become a problem. If a problem arises, however, he has to put the process on the right tracks again.

6.3   How do you become an XP developer?

The success of an XP project depends significantly on the people taking part. The project can only be carried out successfully if the developers can implement well the values and practices of XP. However, a good developer needs to master more than the technical programming tools. We recommend that the developers in an XP team should have a number of other skills:

- Communication skills: Communication between all participants is of vital importance within an XP project. Each developer must be in the position to speak to other developers or to the customers. In pair programming, discussion of designs and implementations is a basic requirement. Without it, pair programming cannot work. Good communication skills are also important for collective design sessions, stand-up meetings and team work.[1]

- Criticism management skills: Developers must be able to criticise and take criticism in order to realise collective ownership, pair programming, and simple design. Each developer in an XP team must be able to say if he or she finds something wrong or bad. If developers cannot take criticism, critical remarks can quickly lead to disputes and

1. Training in communication skills is a very wide topic, which is why we do not go into more detail here. If necessary, you can consult the appropriate literature on the topic of 'group dynamics'.

a sour atmosphere. This must not be allowed to happen. XP is based on the assumption that each developer may voice his or her criticisms, in order to improve the system collectively. Of course, criticisms must be expressed in a constructive way.

- 'Finishing' skills: An XP developer determines to carry out a task with as little cost as possible. He or she only programs as much as is necessary for the task and looks for the simplest way to realise the task (see Section 2.6). This means, however, that an XP developer does not look at smaller or larger tasks but focuses only on the one task and does not 'elaborate' a solution once realised. We often meet developers who come up with a simple solution and then refine, generalise or elaborate it. An XP developer takes care of one task and then goes on immediately to the next. Elaboration is different from refactoring: the project does not need the elaboration but refactorings are always tightly linked with the needs of the project and are carried out to make implementation of requirements easier.

- Programming skills: The proverb 'practice makes perfect' applies to programming. An XP team requires a certain amount of time to get into practice. In order to become a really good XP programmer, you therefore have to program, program and program again. But, do not forget, always program in pairs!

6.4 Management of XP projects

It is often not enough to let the programmers use the XP practices to carry out an operational XP project. A context for the project is needed. The organisation and the management have to involve themselves in the project.

The role of the management is discussed in [Jeffries *et al.* 00]. This role includes providing the optimal working situation for the development team (for example, furnishing the workplace so that the developers can work in pairs). The developers do not have to worry about organising a planning meeting and discussing deadlines as the project manager does that.

It is important that the project manager does not take on the responsibilities of the developers. For example, the project manager is not allowed to estimate the costs in a planning meeting. However, the manager can take over tasks from the developers such as preparing and presenting results for the management.

In many of our projects, the managers may take on other tasks. For example, the management of the customer organisation can influence the prioritisation of the story cards during the planning game. This is strongly associated with splitting the original XP customer into client and user roles, as described in Chapter 3.

On-site customer   An XP project requires an on-site customer, approved by both the development and the customer organisations. If the on-site customer comes under a lot of stress because his organisation does not support him and he has no idea where he will find time for the development project, he will not be a good customer for the project.

Formation of   Contractual agreements are also important for an XP project (see Sec-
contracts   tion 5.3). The management of an XP project is, in our view, responsible for the formation of contracts. The management should keep legal negotiations as far away as possible from the developers. In our experience, it is very unproductive if developers have to attend legal negotiations for days on end. They can use their time a lot more effectively in developing the software system.

6.5 Adaptations of XP

If you use XP for a project, it is not only that the context has to be adapted to XP methods. Often, XP itself has to be adapted to given boundary conditions. This raises the question of how one can adapt and change XP, and what effects this has on the project. In this book we have proposed a number of such adaptations. We concentrate here on the question of which practices can be left out from the start if this is required by the situation.

XP adherents do not approve of adaptations. Many people would state that an XP project is only a 'true' XP project if all the practices are used together; if one omits one of the practices from a development project, then one may no longer call it an XP project. This, of course, is mainly due to the fact that XP is the result of the interaction of the individual practices, principles and values. There is currently much debate about agile development processes; many processes are described as being agile and XP-like, without necessarily earning this description. We have come across some development processes in companies that have features we also see in XP projects; in such cases, the temptation is to describe the process as XP-like. However, writing unit tests alone is insufficient to define a process as XP.

Nevertheless, it seems meaningful for us to take a look at adapted processes (or 'non-XP projects'). It may help you to assess the resultant effects and to profit from experiences with situations where, for example, the management does not allow pair programming or there is no on-site customer available. Whether you still call such a project an XP project or not is up to you. Certainly, projects that take on the basic ideas of XP can normally be carried out better than if one were to renounce XP completely.

Pair programming Pair programming is a technique of XP that does not always find undivided approval. Some developers find that pair programming is only useful for a few 'good' developers, and therefore do without it. In our view, it is possible to eliminate pair programming without destroying the whole process. Of course, without pair programming, collective ownership is more difficult and particular attention has to be paid to ensuring that each developer gets to know and can work with every part of the system.

In our projects, we have managed without pair programming when there is no definite number of programmers present. Many of our developers do not work full-time on a project and so developers inevitably have to work alone. As a rule, this does not cause any problems for future work in the project if it happens for a day or two. In general, programming should always be done in pairs if this is feasible. In particular, during the introductory period, care has to be taken that no developer constantly works on their own, otherwise, code islands that are only understood by one developer inevitably develop.

40-hour week An XP project can also be realised without a 40-hour week, in our view. In our projects, in which part-time programmers form a majority of the team, a 40-hour week cannot be achieved. Other developers may be able to implement a 50-hour week without problems - but not over a longer period of time. The principles that lead to the old technique of the 40-hour week should be applied in such projects: regular overtime makes the employees less efficient and impairs the whole project. In our experience, overtime does not refer to a fixed number of hours, but is strongly dependent on the individual developer. 40 hours a week is however quite a good approximation.

On-site customer We like to have an on-site customer and would not eject one from the project. However, it is not always possible to obtain such a customer. This problem often occurs: workshops and conference discussions deal with this topic and try to find practical solutions. For example, a product manager or a developer could play the role of the customer. It is important in this arrangement, however, that the developers can always question 'the customer' and obtain appropriate answers.

Planning game   As a rule, the planning game has to be adapted to the changed boundary conditions. If the customer is not on-site, the planning game can no longer be carried out in the normal way.

6.6   Typical traps and how to avoid them

There are errors that are made again and again in XP projects. Even in the introductory phase, errors can have serious results. It is not rare for teams to fail during the implementation of XP.

Many errors can be corrected if recognised early. Making errors is part of the learning process and errors can have a positive value, however, one has to be able to recognise errors so that bad habits do not become entrenched. The following list gives some typical errors:

- 'We know what the customer wants and needs.' There is a certain arrogance to this phrase. If the development team is saying this, the feedback from the customers about errors is normally neglected.

- 'It is better to implement story card C before A, even if the customer sets other priorities.' Why then does the customer set priorities at all? Does the development team really know better? No! The prioritisation of the customer helps us to avoid risks. If, for example, we establish that the iteration cannot deal with all story cards after all, we can nevertheless be sure that the most important ones are realised. If the developers change the priorities independently, the worse case is that the release cycle may produce a system which the customer cannot begin to use. If the customer determines the prioritisation, this does not arise.

- Moving deadlines instead of reducing functionality. In projects, it is common practice to simply move deadlines. Frequently, deadlines are moved several times and create an enormous amount of stress during the development. This cannot happen in an XP project. An XP team does not move any deadlines and guarantees that a system can be delivered within the arranged time. At most, the delivered system may not contain the complete functionality. If the customer prioritises the requirements, all the agreed functions are however realised.

- 'I write my classes first and test whether the program does what I want it to do. When it does, I do not write any more test classes. Why should I?' Developers often have this attitude. As a result, fewer and fewer test classes are written. The negative effects of this (see Section 2.5) are not to be underestimated.

- 'Refactorings cannot be broken down.' Instead of smaller steps, refactoring is taken care of in one large step. For this purpose, a branch is created in the source code control system and the change is realised within the new branch. After this, the branch is joined to the main version again. In Section 2.7, we discussed how refactorings *can* be broken down into smaller steps. Initially, we did a lot of refactorings in steps that were too large. In retrospect, we have seen that the refactoring could have been broken down.

- 'Play brilliantly and lose.' In the search for perfect code, developers forget the priorities. They lose themselves in endless design improvements and discussions about possible future requirements. Make sure that this does not happen: XP developers are finishers!

- Continuous integration is carried out without appropriate tests or automatic test support. There is no longer any guarantee that the integrated system carries out all the tests without errors. As a result, there is the danger that the XP process falls to pieces.

- 'Routine tasks need not be programmed in pairs.' Our experience shows that errors can also occur in routine activities. The constant review achieved by a pair when programming is, therefore, sensible for routine activities.

There are certain symptoms ('bad smells') of incorrectly understood or used XP. Every bad smell is signalled by a remark that we hear repeatedly. The fact that someone has made one of the remarks mentioned below is not necessarily proof of a problem but it is worthwhile pricking up your ears and taking a closer look at the facts.

'Make a hand-over.'

If collective responsibility is practised, no hand-over should need to be made if a project member leaves.

'To do so, XXX has to be installed/learnt.'

An XP team takes on the challenge and obtains the necessary abilities and knowledge themselves if necessary. Under no circumstances is an XP team allowed to delay the project because some technical ability or knowledge is not available.

'A proper concept/specification has to be created first.'

At first, developers find that it takes a lot to get used to the absence of a larger conceptual framework in XP projects. Therefore, statements like the above frequently occur at the start of the project. The challenge lies in not falling back into old habits and producing large amounts of paperwork.

'The complexity of the project is underestimated.'

In XP projects, only the current requirements are implemented, and they are implemented in the simplest way that can possibly work. This often seems a little strange to experienced software developers and they fear that the complexity of the project is underestimated. The use of object-oriented technologies, however, achieves a flat expenditure curve and requirements that appear later do not cause any problems.

'For this reason, I prefer to wait until XXX is here again.'

Developers in an XP team take care of the requirements in order. An XP team does not postpone a requirement because a specific developer is not available. If this occurs, collective ownership is not being practised.

6.7   XP games

If you ask developers whether they like their XP work, you usually get a positive answer. Many developers that we know have a lot of fun with XP. Our experience shows that developers work better and faster in a pleasant and friendly working environment. High motivation in a team can clearly increase the productivity of the team as well as the quality of life. It is little wonder that a number of games have been devised for practising and learning the methods and values of the XP process. We introduce two variants here:

eXtreme hour

Peter Merel (see [ExtremeHour]) suggests a one-hour event that illustrates a complete XP project. One or more teams assign their members the roles of customer, coach and developers and carry out a sample project in the context of XP.

Since an actual development project lasts a lot longer than one hour, the eXtreme Hour concentrates on graphical solutions. This means that the customer does not *write down* but *draws* his story cards. The developer's solutions are likewise implemented graphically.

This is difficult if, for example, one wants to build a word processing system. Therefore more physical problems that can be more easily represented graphically are used, for example a coffee machine, a tea machine or a machine that cleans glasses.

An eXtreme Hour is particularly helpful if the team is to get its first impression of XP and is coming into contact with the XP practices and values for the first time. The eXtreme Hour can be used well as an introduction that is also fun. The developers get a good feeling for how the practices work together and how an XP project can run.

Our experience shows that an eXtreme hour can be used to practise the XP methods and to understand how the practices work with one another. In order to carry out an eXtreme Hour, it is imperative to have someone present who has experience with XP and is familiar with the eXtreme Hour.

eXPlanations game

Joshua Kerievsky (see [ExplanationsGame]) suggests a card game. The cards are in three categories: customer, developer and value. On each card there is either the description of a problem or a solution with which one of the problems can be solved. These descriptions are kept short and give sufficient leeway for interpretation (you can find cards on Joshua Kerievsky's Web site and can supplement them with your own cards).

The players can play as individuals or pairs and each team is dealt a set of six cards. Each team in turn displays a card (as a rule, this is a problem card at the start), explains it and describes how the problem (or, later, the solution) looks. The teams then display suitable solution cards and explain how and why their solution card solves the problem described. If the other players are convinced by this, the team can keep both the solution card and the problem card. The winner is the player who has the most cards at the end of the game.

This game can be played by developers that are already familiar with the main features of XP. They can use it to improve their cooperation and learn how solutions for a problem can look. In addition, their team and argumentation skills are also improved.

6.8 Literature

Explanations Game, http://www.industriallogic.com/games/explanations.html

Joshua Kerievsky's Web site gives the instructions for playing this XP game and a set of cards to download.

Extreme Hour, http://c2.com/cgi/wiki?ExtremeHour
  Peter Merel introduces the eXtreme Hour by means of examples

Jeffries, Ron, Anderson, Ann, and Hendrickson, Chet. 2000. *Extreme Programming Installed*. Reading, Massachusetts, Addison-Wesley.
  As well as many other aspects of implementing XP, this book also covers more information on the project manager's role.

Lippert, M., *et al.* 2000. 'JWAM and XP: Using XP for framework development' in *Proceedings of the XP2000 conference*. Cagliari, Sardinia, Italy.
  This article contains some tips on possible adaptations of XP.

Special situations

XP was developed against the background of in-house application development. Since then, XP has been used in various other contexts. We have successfully used XP in a number of projects that deviate from this original schema. In this chapter, we discuss these special project situations and show the aspects in which they deviate from original XP. On the basis of our experience, we give tips on how to deal with specific problems. We anticipate here that XP always has to be adapted to the specific project situation. On the other hand, we have never known of a project that could not profit from XP in some way.

7.1 eXtreme frameworking

Large application systems can hardly be developed today without an appropriate framework. Frameworks allow the developers to reuse designs and implementations. Application developers profit from the experiences that are reified in the framework. As framework developers, we try to pour experiences from different application systems into the framework in order to benefit other application systems. A good framework enables us to develop application systems faster and of a higher quality.

Problem: No on-site customer

The development of a framework is different from an application system in many ways. Framework developers do not necessarily have a direct customer that they can integrate into the project. As a rule, the application projects that are realised on the basis of the framework are the customers of the framework development, but they may be multifaceted. For example, we use the JWAM framework for in-house projects but also license it to external customers. The context of use and thus the requirements of the framework are very varied.

If there is no on-site customer in the framework development, the requirements of the framework may not be taken seriously. Instead, the framework developers assume the functionality that could be useful for application projects and much useless functionality is integrated into the framework.

Solution: Approach application projects as customers

In Section 2.6, we discussed the fact that a framework has to be oriented to the application systems that are built with it. Therefore, we orientate the story cards for the framework towards the requirements that have arisen in application projects. Workarounds that were implemented in application projects can be used to improve the framework. The story cards are written by application developers, who are the main customers of the framework, and prioritised by a group that confers with the person responsible for the application projects. Thus, the requirements of the various application projects can be weighed up against one another.

Requirements from external framework customers are given preferential treatment in order that the licensee of the framework finds his requirements realised as quickly as possible.

Problem:
A stock of
technology

A framework can be used to simplify the realisation of an application system. It does this by containing implementations that can be reused in application systems. Framework developers are therefore inherently at risk of installing a stock of technology. We combat this by only installing a function in the framework if it is actually required for an application. Requirements are written on story cards only when they arise in application projects.

Solution: Use
before
reusing

We should *use* something before it is available in the framework to be *reused*. In our experience, this is a resilient strategy. If we would like to install something in the framework which has not yet been requested in an application project, then a relevant practical example has to be realised. In this case, the functionality is implemented and made available in a special proof-testing area of the framework. The functionality can be delivered to the application projects as a suggestion. If the application projects are interested in it, they write story cards that are implemented in the next release of the framework.

Problem:
Migration costs

There is an inevitable high coupling between applications and framework. If the framework changes, the application systems may have to be changed as well. The adaptations create cost for the application projects, without moving the application forward directly. If the design of the application system is not improved and the functionality is not extended, it is difficult to make a new release of the framework available to the customers. The more frequently the customers obtain new framework releases, the more frequently they have to migrate their applications.

We divide the releases of a framework into two categories. Bug fix releases are delivered as quickly as possible and do not give rise to application migration costs. The XP practice of continuous integration puts us in a good position to produce and deliver bug fix releases. Larger releases of the framework are made after longer time intervals. For us, an interval of six months has proved practical. The application developers thus have time to deal with a new version of the framework and change the application over a period of time. We try to reduce still further the migration costs incurred by customers when they receive new versions of the framework using the following practices:

Solution: Extend
interfaces and use
tools

- Refactorings are divided into two steps. In the first step, we carry out the refactoring (adding new functions, for example) but ensure that the framework can be used in the same way as previously by extending the interfaces. The framework user can, therefore, use his application without changing it and has time until the next release to switch his application over to the new framework. In the second step, we remove old functions and designs. This process does not work for all possible refactorings but, in practice, a large part of the refactorings are covered by it.

- Migration tools are used to changes the applications automatically or, at least, support the application developer in the migration.

Our experience is: We can migrate an operational system to a new framework in one day using these practices.

7.2 Migration of legacy systems

Today, applications are rarely developed from scratch. Much more frequently, existing applications (legacy systems) are replaced or integrated. If the legacy system is replaced, at the very least the old data has to be taken into the new application.

Problems   If the legacy system is to be replaced by the new development, the project team often tries to replace the old system completely and does not provide a gradual migration (the XP practice of small releases is not used). This practice may seem attractive at first glance, but it hides a lot of risks:

- During the redevelopment, the old system is still being developed. There is a danger that the new system, when released, contains less functionality than the old system.

- The lack of small releases means that the possibilities for feedback are reduced. Until the final release, there is no certainty that the new system will be usable.

- The complete development of the new system, as a rule, takes a long time (sometimes several years). During this time, the project team finds it difficult to determine the outward progress of the project. This increases the danger that the project will be stopped during the development.

Solution: Even if the old system is to be completely replaced, small releases should be employed. Our experience shows that this is always possible. Sometimes there are additional costs for the temporary integration of the old system, but they are worthwhile in the end.

In some cases, the old system has to be modified for this kind of integration. Legacy applications normally have no test classes and changes are made more difficult since the danger of side effects is high. Changes to the legacy applications are, however, desirable, if it is easier to convert or integrate the old data.

We recommend that you write unit tests for the units that are to be changed and thus safeguard the changes. Of course, the capabilities of the programming language in which the old system is written have to be taken into account. It is easier to write tests for a system written in C or C++ than for one in Cobol, PL/1, Fortran or Assembler. If one of the latter programming languages is involved, the writing of the tests can become unreasonably time-consuming. In any event, changes to the old system should be carried out in pairs that include a member of the new project team and a developer of the old system.

7.3   E-business applications

E-business applications are a relatively new area for the development of software, so many aspects of this type of application are only partly understood today. There is uncertainty about suitable methods, which leads to e-business applications being developed without a development process. Regular marketing relaunches also lead to development relaunches. Existing applications are rarely developed further.

Problem:
No on-site customers

In the case of e-business applications, the absence of an on-site customer is a big problem. As a rule, it is unclear who will use the system and how. E-business applications are aimed at an enormous, relatively heterogeneous user group. Users of e-business applications cannot give information about the system in usability labs, because of the particular way in which e-business applications are used. Users often use the system from a home computer, in their free time, across a dial-up connection. Using the system, therefore, costs the user time and money and, for example, they are not prepared to wait longer than 10 seconds for the page to load. If you were to let a user work with the system in a usability lab, the situation would be completely different and the results of the usability analyses would be useless.

Solution:
Use small releases

You can partly compensate for the missing customer with small releases. In the case of e-business applications, we should always strive to provide a first version of the system as quickly as possible and then develop it incrementally. The feedback process must also be suitably organised. The users should immediately see how they can give qualitative feedback to the system (through an easily accessible e-mail address, for example) and statistics should be collected from the Web server. The analysis of the Web server data can determine which parts of the system are used and how heavily. In particular, the percentage of the processes that began but did not complete can be established. A high number of aborted processes means that the system is unsuitable for its purpose. The primary cause is usually that the system is unreasonbly complex.

These feedback processes only partly compensate for the customer. It first has to be established what can be assessed and then the feedback can only give general statements such as 'Functionality X is too complex'. Additional functions that would be useful cannot easily be determined in this way. Small releases alone are not enough for the determination of requirements.

Solution: Find 'virtual' customers

Since the users cannot be questioned directly, you must use one or more 'virtual' customers. If you are providing a service for the users (e.g. home banking or calculation of an insurance rate), a conceptual understanding of the user's circumstances is useful. This concept orients the application to the possible circumstances of the user. The released functionality is grouped according to those circumstances and also points to related functions. For example, an insurance company may have a concept of 'starting a family'. In this context, the system may offer certain products, such as extending existing third-party insurance for the spouse, life assurance and an educational savings policy. As a rule, the user's circumstances can be determined relatively easily with the help of the company, which has direct contact with the customer. Insurance companies typically have a good insight into the circumstances of their customers.

7.4 Product development

Software is developed for different purposes. We frequently encounter in-house development carried out by larger companies that have their own development departments. In contrast to this, some software development projects have a product as their goal.

The product development has a different context from an in-house software project and has to be dealt with in a different way. The change in context influences the development process. XP cannot always be carried out in the same way, we can adapt it appropriately for product development.

As a rule, a product is not developed for a specific customer. For the user, products have the advantage that they are cheaper to buy than custom-made software. For the development organisation, the product can be sold to many customers without incurring additional development costs.

Problem: An XP development process requires a customer that can be questioned about the application range and can prioritise story cards. In a normal XP project, the developer receives feedback from the customers through small releases and acceptance tests. These elementary properties of an XP project cannot be directly implemented in the development of a product. Can XP be implemented at all in this context?

Solution:
Use product manager as the customer

The project organisation must replace the on-site customer adequately. If the on-site customer is simulated in a suitable way, the negative effects on the other practices are reduced. A product manager can take on the role of the on-site customer. He gives the development team feedback, writes and prioritises story cards, and defines acceptance tests. The product manager as a rule is from the development company. This makes him an ideal candidate for the role of customer, since the development team always has access to him. The task of the product manager is very demanding in such an environment. He has to be able to put himself in the shoes of the future customer in order to judge the product and uncover possible weaknesses.

The development of a product is only rarely complete after its first delivery. Frequently, further requirements or desired changes arise when the product is put into practice by its users. It is obvious, therefore, that the product manager cannot completely replace the 'true' customer; he is an aid for the development team, not a complete substitute.

It does not, however, help the development team even once there are users with experience of the product. There may be a large number of users and the team still does not have direct access to a user who can take on the role of the on-site customer. However, the product manager can now collect feedback from the users and pass it on to the team. The project manager thus learns more about the perceptions and work situations of the users and his own future estimates regarding the product become more closely oriented with those of the real users. This improves the quality of the feedback that the product manager can give to the development team.

7.5 Outsourcing

Development projects are more and more frequently subcontracted (or 'outsourced') to external software development companies. Outsourcing may be for a complete application system or for the programming of components to be integrated into other developments.

Since software development is not as a rule aimed at copying existing applications, but at the development of new systems or components, at the start of the project it is often not certain how the outcome will look.

The project team has the task of sketching out requirements and implementing them suitably. XP does this using an iterative method with small releases to assess intermediate results and discover potential problems early on.

Problem: Ill-defined outcome

When development is subcontracted to an external partner, the commissioning cannot specify exactly how the expected outcome will look. This is a problem for a fixed-price time and materials contract. In this case, the expected outcome has to be described accurately so that a court can make a clear judgement if there is a dispute.

Solution: Develop acceptance tests

If only sophisticated algorithmic parts of the system are to be subcontracted externally, a specification of the expected results can be made via tests. These can, if necessary, be a component of the contract. The customer would write the tests and the contractor would write classes that satisfy the tests. Using a suitable test tool, the customer and the contractor can both check whether the developed classes satisfy the tests. If the contractor also proceeds according to XP, the first classes can be made available after a short period and both the contractor and the customer can control the number of tests that are carried out. The tests are used as acceptance tests, even if they are implemented as unit tests. If the classes are submitted to the customer, the original acceptance tests are reused as unit tests.

If a complete application is to be implemented, acceptance tests can also be used. However, the situation is a lot more challenging. Applications usually have a user interface that is ergonomic and supports the user and cannot be defined with justifiable effort in acceptance tests. Acceptance tests are aimed fundamentally at the functionality of the system. With this constraint, acceptance tests can be implemented in the same way as unit tests. However, the expense of defining acceptance tests gets larger the closer the test comes to the interface. It is thus more difficult to write an acceptance test for a text editor if the test has to establish not only that texts are saved and loaded, but also that they are displayed in a formatted way. The accuracy of the specification has to be weighed against the cost. However, the central element remains the specification by acceptance tests, in contrast to data models, descriptions of internal program sequences, etc.

Solution: Define technical standards

Another problem concerns the technical quality of the software. Acceptance tests cannot determine how the internal structure of the software is created. However, there are rules of thumb for the architecture of object-oriented systems, which at least provide a guide for good design. For example, a common rule is 'avoid cyclical use relations between classes'. In practice, the slavish following of this rule can lead to unnecessarily complicated system design. Contractors and customers may agree that cyclical use relations may occur within a Java package in the context of a design pattern.

Customers and contractors can use these guidelines to define a common measurement of quality. If there is any doubt, a third project partner with competence in the area of architecture and quality assessment can check the set of quality measurements at pre-agreed intervals. The result of the investigation is made available to the contractor as well as the customer. The contractor can thus stop violations of the agreed standards.

7.6   Certification of development processes

ISO-9000 and the Capability Maturity Model (CMM) both certify development processes. Certification should guarantee that a development process meets a particular standard of quality. For this reason, certification behaves 'virulently'. If a software developer relies on subcontractors, he can only establish a quality standard for his development process if his subcontractors are also certified. As a consequence, software manufacturers from time to time feel that it is necessary to be certified without seeing a direct use for this. At the same time, the general question about the sense of such certification is pushed into the background. A certificate may only be necessary for economic considerations.

Certification seems to contradict the ideas of XP. ISO-9000 demands a certain formalisation and this suppresses XP's flexibility during the development. Thick files, in which every small detail of the development process is written down accurately, are often the result of a ISO-9000 certification. Thick files are quite definitely not in the spirit of XP.

But a thick file is not *necessary* for an ISO-9000 certification. This assumption is sometimes spread by companies with ISO-9000 certification. In fact, ISO-9000 merely demands that the development process is comprehensible. XP already does this in its basic form by determining exactly which practices are used in which way. For this reason, XP should be certified if some things are put into concrete terms. This hypothesis is supported by the fact that there is at least one certified XP-like development process.

7.7 Literature

Gamma, Erich. 1992. *Objektorientierte Software-Entwicklung am Beispiel von ET++*. Berlin, Heidelberg, Springer-Verlag.
ET++ was one of the first larger frameworks.

Lewis, T. 1995. *Object-Oriented Application Frameworks*. Greenwich, Manning Publications.
This is a collection of standard essays on the topic of frameworks.

Lippert, M., *et al.* 2000. 'JWAM and XP: Using XP for framework development' in *Proceedings of the XP2000 conference*. Cagliari, Sardinia, Italy.

Roock, S. 2000. 'eXtreme Frameworking: How to aim applications at evolving frameworks' in *Proceedings of the XP2000 conference*. Cagliari, Sardinia, Italy.
This article discusses the problem of migration to new framework versions that are developed in a highly cyclical process.

Project reports

In this book, we have referred several times to XP project experiences that we have collected over the last three and a half years. In this chapter, we describe four projects in detail. We have selected projects so that as many different aspects as possible are mentioned. One project focuses on a short period of development (three months); the expense for another is relatively large (approximately 300–400 person months). Some are complete in-house projects; in others we have merely supported the developers of our customers.

In each of the examples we highlight only the parts of each project that are different from pure XP theory, since we have already described the XP practices in detail. If a project report, for example, does not contain any remarks on continuous integration, we have used this practice without special experiences or adaptations.

Many projects have adapted the practices. Sometimes not all XP practices have been used. Some of the projects would definitely not be described as pure XP projects, by the forefathers of XP who repeatedly emphasise that a project is only a true XP project if all values and practices are used in cooperation. Even if our projects do not implement the 'pure theory', we nevertheless describe them as XP projects since, in our opinion, they all have typical XP characteristics. The XP team may forgive us for this.

Apart from the JWAM framework development, we discuss all the projects anonymously. The names used have nothing to do with the real project names.

8.1 Project Kermit

Context

This project was one of the first customer projects in which we used XP. The project was the first object-oriented project in a number of attempted extensions to a central host computer system. The customer was the German branch office of an international service company with a central data processing system in another European country.

Aim of the project

The aim of the project was to implement country-specific procedures involved in processing complex terms for motor vehicle repurchase contracts that were previously processed using Microsoft Excel.

Resources

Initially, we had two developers available to us for approximately two days a week in order to determine an initial technical understanding in a pre-analysis of only two months. After this, an estimate for a fixed-price quotation for the system development also had to be given. Three developers developed the first core system over a period of approximately six months for about two to three days a week (about 120 person days of cost in total).

The role of the user department in the project was to be available for the developers as a partner with whom they can carry out interviews and reviews. A particular motor vehicle repurchase contract type was made a priority at the very start. Further contract types were programmed at irregular intervals.

Challenge   The main challenge of the project was including the complex technical connections.

XP use

In this project, we used pair programming and acceptance testing. The tests were useful for trying out, by means of practical examples, the complex models of the requirements of the contracts. Pair programming and collective ownership reduced the truck factor so that the loss of a developer for three months (due to a slipped disc) did not jeopardise the success of the project.

Continuous integration and refactoring   Since only three developers worked on the project and only part-time, the work on the code was organised so that only two developers were working on it at the same time. This made it possible to integrate regular changes without much technical cost. No organisational conflicts were incurred during the editing of the code. It was striking, though, that we first had to learn to break down larger refactorings into sufficiently small modifications so that every evening there was an operational system available. This did not happen every evening at the start of the project.

On-site customer, planning game   Because of the fixed-price nature of the contract and a sequence of priorities that was already relatively clear in the preliminary stages, the planning game was not employed. If there were any questions during the development, the employees from the user department were always there to help the developers by e-mail and by telephone. The size of the project would not have allowed for a user to be there all of the time.

Metaphors   The users had had previous experiences with failed IT projects in which developers had been 'dazzled' with incomprehensible user jargon. From the beginning our standing was very good, because we were using terms and concepts that were familiar to the users. This was increased even further when we found a metaphor (the 'translucent base contract') with which the complex subcontracts were reproduced in the software system and which was easy to understand. The implementation of the metaphor involved the formation of subcontracts that could be seen through the criteria of the basic contract (in grey). Each criterion could be varied specifically for the subcontract.

Short releases and prototypes The first versions that were delivered were not a finished product that could have been used. Rather, they were prototypes that we used to establish a collective idea of the future system with the users. In retrospect, we could have tried to make versions from these prototypes that could have been used earlier in order to obtain feedback from the users about its productivity a lot more quickly. This would, however, have required substantial installation costs and on-site support.

Coding conventions The project was implemented by JWAM developers using JWAM coding conventions.

Evaluation

The project was seen by both the customers and ourselves as a big success and we acquired further large projects from this customer.

A fixed price is a tough restriction for XP projects, particularly with regards to the planning game. In the project described here, it was not too important because of the small size of the project. Towards the end of the project, and shortly before it was made available to the customer, an enquiry was made as to whether we would be able to keep to the estimated cost. We discovered that this was not the case and honestly reported to the customer that we had overrun the budget by about 10%. The customer allowed us an overdraft of approximately 10% of the expense, which is rather unusual for fixed-price projects. We took this as an indication that they were very happy with our work.

In XP it is important for the developers, during the course of the project, to learn from the users, to adopt their language and to tackle their tasks and the associated task handling by means of the supporting software system.

8.2 Project Gonzo

Context

Our customer in this project was a software house in Germany that wanted to create a software system for processing complex, net-like structures. The software allows its users to design and explain these diagrams. It incorporates Web applications and associated back office functionality, which can also be used with a Web front end. In addition to the Web technology, we also had to focus on the support of business processes.

Aim of the project The aim of the project was to develop the graphical tools with which net structures and their underlying functionalities can be designed and developed for our customer. A system developed with the graphical tools was made operational through a special server that was developed by our customer.

The project was relatively unusual: two programming teams worked on the software system at different times and in different places. In our account, 'the project' refers only to the part of the total project in which our team developed the graphical tools.

Our customer intended to demonstrate the software in an international customer and investor presentation at a time which had already been agreed. The tools therefore had to be in a demonstratable state by this time and the deadline could not be moved.

At the start of the project, the customer had merely provisional ideas about how the system should look. We therefore began to develop a prototype in order to create a more accurate idea of the system with our customer. During the course of the prototype development, we identified a number of further possible difficulties and risks that we estimated using further laboratory prototypes. After about two months, the customer decided to develop the system and product development began straight away as there were only three months to the presentation.

Resources   In the first month, we made 20 programming days per week available for the customer. In the following two months, we increased this to 25 person days per week. We achieved this number of programming days through a team of an average of seven people, who did not all work full-time. Therefore we could increase the number of programming days per month without taking on additional developers in the project.

XP use

Prototype   Our team chose a suitable XP process for developing the graphical tools,
development   using all the XP practices. At the start of the project, we allocated more time for the development of the prototype than is normal in XP with spike solutions. This seemed to make sense since the customer's ideas about the future system were so unclear that no useful story cards could have been created. The prototypes allowed us to find a suitable metaphor for the total system and could therefore form the basis for the creation of the story cards.

Only three developers were involved in the prototyping and, in principle, the XP practices were already being used. There were slight adaptations to the practice of the on-site customer. The technical analysis was carried out by one of our developers with a representative of the customer. The developer and the customer representative worked out the problems for the prototypes. These problems were the basis for the story cards which we then implemented in-house. The developer who had already carried out the analysis for the customer was available to the other developers to talk about things that were unclear.

Experienced developers We consciously put together a team for the product development in which almost all the programmers had experience with XP. Because of this, we did not have any difficulties in installing the XP values in the team.

On-site customer The story cards were written by our customers and were estimated by us. Since we were in a different city to the customer, we did not have access to an on-site customer. We got around this problem by calling them up whenever we had a question. This situation was made easier as there was a nominated contact to whom we put our questions and who made all the important decisions concerning the preparation and prioritisation of the story cards.

Continuous integration We made particularly intensive use of continuous integration and it was not rare to make 20 integrations per day. With two to three programming pairs per day, we developed the system in small steps.

Refactoring We developed the product from the prototypes. The elementary practice of refactoring was an indispensable tool for this.

Small releases The release cycles in the project were kept unusually short, even for an XP project. Since the product development basically had to be completed within three months, we dispensed with iterations within the release cycles. It would have made no sense to give a release to our customer at the end of the three months or even once a month in order to obtain feedback. We were instructed to obtain feedback in much shorter intervals so that we could react to it as quickly as possible. We therefore delivered at least one release per week to the customer.

Evaluation

The development of a prototype at the start of the project proved to be very profitable. The customer and ourselves could get a good idea of the system to be developed. The customer's developers were also able to take part in the discussions and were involved from the start of the development process.

Prototype development In this case, the prototype was suitable for creating a common vision of the product. We could use it as a basis for the product and so it was not a throw-away prototype. There were two reasons for this: the prototype developers were very experienced and the JWAM framework made it possible for us to develop the prototype quickly and on a solid and sustainable architecture. The architecture made it possible to move into the product development without any breaks.

Refactoring Nevertheless, we developed the product in small steps and with each small step improved the design. Refactorings were necessary and we learned that refactorings cannot be put off for too long. At some points, we put off refactorings because of time pressure. In the end, it was very clear in various parts of the system that we should not have done that. We made intensive use of refactoring for one part of the system and it was always easy to develop and errors were easy to find. In another part of the system, we put off refactoring and noticed (even within the three months) that this part of the system was not so elegant and was not so easy to develop.

JWAM
Integration Server

During the product development, the JWAM Integration Server particularly proved itself. We could realise 20 and more integrations a day without any problems. Sometimes, developers within our team had to test and develop in the place of the on-site customer and the Integration Server also supported this situation very well. Considerable integration costs rarely occurred and the development was not slowed down at any point.

Continuous
integration

Continuous integration was very profitable for the project. We were able to react flexibly to the wishes of the customer and were also able to provide the customer with a completely operational system that represented the up-to-date status of the development at any time. We were able to deliver several releases a week and even two in one day without taking any risks.

Small releases

Small releases had a positive effect on the project. We were able to have intensive discussions with the customer about the releases. Missing properties or misunderstandings were recognised early. Within the development team, the short time between releases did not prove to be disruptive. By implementing continuous integration, all developers were sure that the release was going to be possible.

Incomplete test
coverage

The delivery of releases was only impaired by incomplete test coverage. In the beginning, we did not consistently write the tests first. During the course of the project this led to the unit test coverage remaining at a relatively low level. This was made painfully obvious during the course of the project. For over two weeks, we didn't notice that a function of the system was no longer working because there was no corresponding unit test for it. When we finally needed this function on-site for the customer we were faced with a problem: we had to get it running again on-site. The cause of the problem was found quickly (data was saved using Java Serialization and we had added classes that were not `Serializable`). Although the errors could be found quickly, we needed a certain amount of time to eliminate them. This situation would have been avoided if we had a unit test.

We came to the conclusion that we would pay more attention to the unit tests in the next project. We realised that it is important to implement them from the start. Testing first helps to provide good test coverage.

However, we could not have written unit tests for all the aspects of the highly-interactive tools. It is difficult to cater for the graphical front end of the tools in test cases. We have, therefore, clearly separated presentation, interaction and function, which simplifies unit tests considerably. In most projects, covering the presentation part of the tool completely with unit tests has a high cost.

External quality assessment   Towards the end of our development projects, we measure our source code using software metrics developed for us by our partners at the Technical University of Cottbus. This results in a detailed report about the weak points of a system. In contrast to many software-metric approaches, these metrics do not claim to be an absolute measure of quality. They do however show extremes in the system, which can help to improve the system. The quality model thus helps to incorporate some quality requirements into these readings.

In this project, the report did not show any great weak points in the system. This strengthens even more our impression that we have refactored and improved the system over and over again in the course of the development. These software metrics have proved successful in a number of projects.

Length of the project   The use of XP for this project seemed worthwhile, although the project lasted a relatively short time. The XP community is still discussing whether XP is really worthwhile for such short projects. We were able to develop effectively with XP in these three months and received feedback from our customers after short periods of time. Since priorities shifted repeatedly within the three months and requirements were detailed, we would not have been able to react adequately without an appropriately adjusted development process.

The speed of the development was certainly not based on XP alone. The development team consisted of experienced Java developers who were familiar with design patterns, frameworks, and XP. We therefore did not need to take any training costs into account. If the team had had to learn XP first, the situation certainly would have looked different.

8.3 Project Scooter

Context

In this project, we advised a German insurance company about object-oriented technologies and processes, and provided additional developers. The planning of the project began at the end of 2000 and the project started officially on 1 January 2001. The end of the project is planned for the year 2004.

Aim of the project   The aim of the project was to standardise existing systems and to support new requirements, in particular in the area of multi-channel ability. The standardisation of the existing systems was not only for technical reasons. Technical application factors made the separation of definitions of general insurance products more difficult. Such divisions should cover complete areas of life, e.g. starting a family, with a bundle of insurance policies.

The existing host systems were developed against the background of in-house processing. They were optimised for the transfer of data from an application form into the system. This optimisation was inadequate for the new channels (Internet customers, brokers).

The main emphasis changed several times during the course of the project. Whilst the redevelopment of the host system was the initial focus of the development, the support of additional channels (Internet customers and brokers) was given higher priority.

Resources   Initially, we worked with one and a half external consultants. This number was increased to two after six months. Internally, approximately a dozen employees were assigned to the project. Of these, however, few were available to the project 100% of the time. Furthermore, knowledge about Java, object-orientation and modern methods was only available sporadically. At first the insurance company provided only two programmers (one person for 100% of the time and two people for about 50% each). The project was also assigned a project manager, three employees responsible for the company's workflow, two employees from the product area, a data modeller and an administrator. The division of work according to specialist areas has broken down more and more so that today there is essentially only a division between developers and users. Through internal training and education, the development capacity in the insurance company has increased to approximately seven people.

XP use

Introducing XP   It is rather unusual to use XP in an insurance company and it quickly became clear that XP was attractive to a portion of the developers. To other developers and the management, XP often seemed rather daunting at first – partially due to its name.

We therefore did not introduce XP as a whole; we introduced the individual practices as necessary. We regarded XP as a toolbox from which we could use practices that addressed concrete, recognisable problems. If, at the end of the process, XP is not complete but the project works well, what is the point in dogmatically introducing the additional practices? We introduced the XP practices gradually and today they are all in use.

Prototype development   First of all, a couple of small prototypes (spike solutions) were developed in an exploration phase in order to clarify important application-specific and technical problems:

- An implementation prototype gave information about whether a desktop interface was necessary for the official in charge or whether a Web interface was sufficient.

- An architecture prototype tested whether the intended service architecture was suitable for setting up different front ends for the same technical functionality. This prototype was merged with the implementation prototype.

- A performance prototype clarified whether the speed of the system was sufficient.

The project required almost six weeks to 'tune up'. During this time, the prototypes were created by one of the consultants. The prototypes confirmed the assumptions: officials in charge needed a desktop interface, the service architecture was sustainable, and both data models and object models performed well enough in their main features.

Stage plan On the basis of the prototypes, a first rough project plan (a stage plan) was created. This contained stages for the total system that were, respectively, one and three months long. Initially, we provided the stages with dates for only the first 18 months. The prioritisation of the stages took place on the basis of the priorities achieved in the project. This plan was submitted to the IT manager, who accepted it. At this point, he only cared about finishing the project before 2004. The sequence of the developed components was initially left up to the project team.

Small releases With the stage plan, the notion of small releases also entered the project. The discussion about small releases were not easy at the start of the project. It was often argued that the host system had to be replaced as a whole and therefore small releases could not be achieved. From the discussion, however, the possibilities of implementing small releases crystalized on the approach of using the old and the new systems in parallel for a limited period of time. We not only oriented the planning of the individual stages to technical priorities, but also defined them so that in their work situations the users had to switch between the old and new systems as rarely as possible.

Stand-up meetings We introduced daily stand-up meetings very early on. We met up every day at 11:45 for a maximum of 15 minutes. The rules that we have already described applied to those meetings: keep it short, no discussions, limit it to the essentials.

User integration As well as the requirements, technical objectives also played an important part in the project. Therefore, the project team had a number of contact people. The IT manager is responsible for the technical objectives and each user group has to take into account specific requirements. Each release of the system is the focus of the user group and a representative acts for this user group in the planning game.

The planning game and story cards   On the basis of the stage plan, the user representative wrote story cards for the coming stage with the developers, if necessary. Depending on the main focus of the iteration, the planning game was played with one user representative and the stories were estimated in an abstract unit (valued from one to five). At the end of each iteration, the number of units processed were calculated and the productivity of the team was calculated in units per week. The calculated productivity is the basis for the planned capacity of the next iteration. Figure 8.1 shows the gradient of the productivity in the project. The peak in iteration 3 is probably an allocation error explained by the fact that we worked initially without an explicit iteration concept; the first three iterations were reconstructed on the basis of the dates on the story cards. The fall in the productivity in iteration 8 and the recovery in iteration 9 is notable. We had put off a large refactoring for too long and made up for it in iteration 8. The increased productivity in iteration 9 shows that the refactoring was sensible.

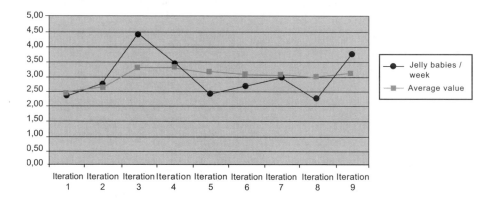

Figure 8.1   Development of productivity in the Scooter project

The chart shows that the average productivity is very even. Just to be on the safe side, when planning the next iteration, we calculate the value for the next iteration as average of the low value from the last iteration and the measured average.

Programming in pairs for training

We introduced pair programming, unit tests and continuous integration in parallel with the story cards. From the start, pair programming was thought of as being a training practice which could be used to permanently integrate the OO and Java experience of the external consultant into the team. This showed that pair programming is only suitable for hands-on training if the difference in abilities between the two partners is not too great. Pairs in which experienced Java developers work with newcomers to OO and Java were not proved to be sensible. The project progress tended to be negligible as the experienced developers spent almost all of their time training their partner. Despite this, the newcomers learned very little as they felt under pressure and were unable to take the time they needed to understand the concepts. The XP community calls this kind of situation 'Pair Teaching' instead of pair programming.

We therefore divided the team of developers into a group of developers with an average to large amount of knowledge and a group of newcomers who worked on a mini project that was part of a future project stage. The newcomers had an incentive to develop this part well so that it can be used later but if the mini project failed, the whole project was not in danger. The experienced developers could have redeveloped these functionalities for the appropriate project stage. In the mini project, the developers worked in pairs with alternating partners.

Putting the development pairs together was a bit of a nuisance. The employees in the project were from different department groups and worked flexitime. In the insurance company, it was normal for each department group to have breakfast together in the canteen. In order not to overtax the canteen, the groups did not all go at the same time. This meant that some of the employees started working at 7 a.m. and left at 2.30 p.m. Other employees were not available until around 9.30 a.m. and we could not begin effective pair programming until about 10 a.m., by which time some employees have already used up almost half of their working day. This problem was present beyond the project but there is no solution as yet. Since the very early starters were in a minority, the damage was limited. Developers without partners work on improving tests and documenting the system.

Unit tests and continuous integration with VisualAge

Unit tests and continuous integration began well but were hindered at one point by VisualAge for Java. VisualAge does not store its files in the file system but in a repository. Because of this, it is easy to release changed files from the central repository. It is however not easy to force the execution of unit tests. This led to the unit tests being executed too rarely and the code basis in the central repository frequently did not conform to the tests. We addressed this issue with two mechanisms: an e-mail was sent to all developers twice a day (at 10 a.m. and 4 p.m.) to remind them to carry out all tests; and a copy of the central repository was made every Monday after running all the unit tests. The version that existed on Monday was available on the server so that, for example, the project manager could access it and present it at any time. This version was also available for users to test, which proved worthwhile, particularly towards the end of a project stage.[1]

Coding conventions

After the first project stage, it was clear that there was a lack of coding conventions. The developers had different backgrounds and very different programming styles. We therefore set up coding conventions for the project based on Sun's Java Code Conventions and on the specific properties of VisualAge.

Metaphors

The project is based on the JWAM framework. This led to the first rough metaphors being domain values, material, tool and service provider. The metaphors were detailed further. The material product component and the convention component are at the core of the system. Depending on the channel, these two metaphors are supplemented further. The employees of the product area process product components with a special tool, the product definer.

Simple design and refactoring

Introducing simple design took a long time and is not completely over yet. Due to experiences with conventional technologies (Cobol, etc.) it was not always easy to convey to the project members that designs could be changed and enriched later on. The team has basically accepted that simple design is meaningful but they need to practise it. This also applies to refactoring. Not all project members can yet break down refactorings into small enough chunks so that they can be carried out in a few minutes. It seems intuitive to find pairs for such refactorings so that one of the partners is an experienced developer.

Collective ownership

Collective ownership was never a problem as far as the source code was concerned. The communication within the team was always so good that there were no problems with coordination either. At the start, collective ownership was hindered somewhat by VisualAge because the team had first to learn how to use VisualAge for this.

Tuning workshops

In the end, we set up tuning workshops. At the end of each iteration, the developers sat together for a few hours in order to discuss problems that had arisen. Possible solutions were discussed and decided upon so that they could be used for the next iteration.

---

1. The project eliminated this problem by using Eclipse, CVS, and a special integartion guard now instead of VisualAge for Java.

Evaluation

The project has completed its first stages. The XP practices have all been introduced and work well, although there are, of course, more optimisation possibilities.

XP has proved absolutely successful. For insurance company employees who do not work on the project, it sometimes seems strange that we are using XP. In particular, the way of planning and the small releases take a lot of getting used to. On the other hand, it has become apparent that the project delivers high quality results within an agreed time, which needs as much getting used to. The in-house atmosphere towards the project is generally positive.

We are now talking about describing the method in an internal project management handbook and using it as a model for all other OO projects. This raises important questions for the future. After all, XP is based on four values (see Section 1.1) that cannot be 'set up'. Values have to be learnt, experienced and practised. It is an interesting challenge to find a way both to distribute XP throughout the company and to make sure that the project proceeds according to XP and practises the XP values.

8.4 Project JWAM

Context

The JWAM framework emerged from an initiative of scientific employees and students at the University of Hamburg. The development began in 1997. Today, the JWAM framework is used professionally by IT Workplace Solutions GmBH (IT WPS) for some development projects and is licensed to customers.

Aim of the project
The aim is to have a framework available for Java development in the context of research and teaching the Tools and Materials approach. During the course of the professionalisation, the support of commercial development projects was added as a further aim.

Resources
IT WPS is mainly financed by projects. In the case of any conflict, the project business is prioritised higher than the JWAM framework. This has led to development resources for the JWAM framework being almost nonexistent. When we realised this, we established the concept of JWAM sprints: once a month, a sprint takes place in which all employees should participate. A minimum of resources is provided but the developers still end up being trained in working with the framework. Since time pressures are still prevalent in projects, not all employees take part in the JWAM sprints. On average, approximately eight to ten employees take part in a sprint.

XP use

We first heard about XP at the end of 1998 in conferences. At the start of 1999 we began to implement some of the XP practices. At this point in time, JWAM consisted of over 400 classes and no test classes.

Pair programming

First of all we introduced pair programming, unit tests and simple design. We found out that pair programming sounded simple, but was not always easy to put into practice. To begin with, we stuck with our normal desk arrangement, with drawers on either side. This meant that the reviewer ended up sitting behind the programmer and could not participate as strongly as desired. As a change in roles of the two partners was connected with an elaborate swapping of seats, at the start we only switched roles once a day (after lunch). We solved this problem by getting hold of tables without drawers and positioning the tables differently in the room (see Section 2.8).

Unit tests and simple design

The development of the missing unit tests was not trivial and took about 18 months. It turned out that it was useful not only to write the missing unit tests for all classes but also to carry out simple design. For each class, we thought about whether to write the unit test or delete the class. In this way, about 50% to 75% of the original classes were removed from the framework. Almost all of the remaining classes were drastically simplified so that they could be tested at a realistic cost. Neither the removal of the classes nor the simplification had a negative influence on the actual functional range of the framework. This makes it clear that a big stock of technology had collected in the JWAM framework.

In this context, we had to deal with conflict between the simplicity of the framework and the best possible support for the development of applications. The former led to a very small framework and the latter to a very large one. We resolved the conflict by introducing a distinction between the JWAM core (at the moment about 100 operational classes) and JWAM components (between 10 and 50 classes in each component). The additional components better support application development without unnecessarily burdening the core. This keeps the internal structure of the JWAM framework concise while making the framework for application development more manageable. Application developers can first of all learn the JWAM core and can extract the necessary components at a later stage.

Collective ownership

The JWAM framework was developed classically with individual code ownership. Consequently, certain parts of the framework were known only by individual developers. During the course of pair programming these 'dark corners' have been eliminated. At the same time we have introduced collective ownership which has made the development process a lot more flexible as now anyone can change anything.

Continuous integration   The next XP practice we dealt with was continuous integration. First of all, we used a second physical computer as an integration machine on which the up-to-date state of the framework should always be available and operational. Changes were to be integrated onto it as quickly as possible. This method caused a lot of problems. A connection to the integration machine was not always available during the development of the JWAM framework because we often worked on it at home or in a hotel room. Furthermore, a framework, in contrast to an application, is not directly executable. Therefore, versions on the integration machine were not 100% operational. We tried to control this problem with checklists. In each integration, the whole checklist was to be gone through to make sure that the integrated portfolio was operational. Unfortunately, this took two to four hours, which led to a set of changes being collected before the integration was tackled.

We used these problems as an opportunity to have a student project develop software for the continuous integration. The result was the JWAM Integration Server, which we have since used for all of our in-house projects. The Integration Server encapsulates version control and makes sure that only the classes that do not fail the tests can be integrated. It can also be accessed across the Internet from anywhere through an encoded connection.

We also started to write tests for the interactive parts of the framework. To do this we used the concept of dummy types for the interface elements. We also programmed a number of examples of different sizes as a component of the framework. These examples compensate for the disadvantage that the framework cannot be executed.

All these measures together meant that we could use continuous integration without problems and that the common code basis is always operational. A JWAM integration currently lasts six to seven minutes for approximately 2,500 classes (with tests and example classes). We are working to reduce this time even further.

Refactoring   We began the refactoring at the same time as the unit tests, but refactorings failed where we wanted to run them without unit tests. It took us a long time to learn how to break down a refactoring so that it could be run in just a few minutes. For example, in 1999 we completely rebuilt a JWAM component. There were doubts that the refactorings could be broken down into as small chunks as we wanted and the complete component was de-coupled and developed in its own sector. The reconfiguration of the component took several weeks and the integration took just as long and was extremely painful. In this case – and in all other similar cases – we could see afterwards that breaking it down into smaller refactorings would have been possible and sensible.

This is one of the reasons why the Integration Server implements an optimistic cooperation model and why files cannot be locked. There is a race between the developers, who carry out smaller refactorings and can therefore integrate faster. Everyone knows that the winner of the conflict is the one that has integrated first. Those who follow have to merge with the changes of the winner.

Small releases

We put out new JWAM releases every six months. For the developer, this time can be drastically reduced without any problems. We can deliver a new version after every sprint. If particular new functionality is urgently required in our project, the project immediately uses the corresponding JWAM intermediate version.

The main argument against reducing the length of release cycles is based on the migration costs for the application developer. We have consciously chosen not to go out of our way to keep framework versions downwardly compatible. This would accelerate the aging process of the framework too much. As a consequence, applications have to be migrated when a new framework is made available. At the moment, we do not want our customers to experience these migration costs more than twice a year. We are however working on better support of migration in order to be able to reduce the release cycles.

On-site customer and planning game

The on-site customer and the planning game are two practices that we were able to adapt for the framework at our first attempt. Since the framework developers used JWAM in their own projects, these practices did not seem absolutely necessary at first. This lead to problems, however, because the interests of the sales department and the JWAM licensees were not always adequately taken into account. Recently, we have been more and more successful. We have introduced a distinction between story and task cards for the development of frameworks. Task cards are written by any developer and first and foremost deal with refactorings. Story cards come from the JWAM sales department, our own application projects and JWAM licensees. The planning game focuses on the story cards. When appropriate, a cost buffer is reserved in which additional cards can be taken care of. The task cards are included in the plans by the JWAM organisation's team. If possible, they are fastened to story cards.

For the planning game itself, we use an asynchronous variation since many of our developers and consultants mainly work at the customer's workplace and it would be impossible to find a time to have a planning game as a group. The sales department, application projects and licensees give each story card up to three points. The story cards with the highest number of points is given the highest priority by the JWAM team.

Metaphor

The JWAM framework supports the application developers according to WAM, in which the tool, automaton and material metaphors have priority. The examples in JWAM are naturally designed according to these metaphors. We cannot yet say that the whole framework was designed according to a few metaphors and we are not sure that this would have been sensible. In some components, certain metaphors appear repeatedly. In the JWAM core if the need arises, some small design patterns can be found.

Coding conventions

JWAM coding conventions have been around since the start of the development. They are only a few pages long and are also used for application projects. We update the coding conventions as the need arises.

Sustainable pace

Since the JWAM development is essentially organised in sprints, this practice is subordinate. A sprint lasts for two to four days, so it lasts normally for about 16 to 32 hours. In the week in which the sprint takes place, the 40 hours working time of an average developer can be exceeded. However, since the sprints only take place once a month, there is enough time for recovery before the next sprint.

Evaluation

We collected our first XP experiences with the JWAM framework. We were able to try out a lot of things and have therefore learnt a lot. However, the effects of this learning were relatively expensive because of the time that was taken. We would therefore recommend that beginners use an experienced in-house XP coach to obtain more XP know-how.

Although the learning was relatively expensive in the beginning, the introduction and use of XP have proved this exercise to be worthwhile as far as the process and product are concerned. Despite its age, the framework is in good health and, in contrast to many other frameworks, it has not become a rigid, inflexible monster. Instead, the manageability and the functionality have been steadily developed so that its use in the development of applications is permanently growing.

Since the framework has been licensed to customers in large numbers and the number of new IT WPS employees has grown, the documentation of the framework has become an important topic of discussion. So far, we have only invested as much money in documentation as we have needed ourselves. This investment now has to be increased. This does not, however, represent a problem: the requirement for documentation is a requirement like any other, which is recorded on story cards and prioritised in the planning game.

Evaluation and outlook

9

9.1 Evaluation

We have been implementing XP since 1999. Since then, we have run all projects where the practice could be employed with XP. This means that we have used in the real world, depending on the context of the project, the adaptations introduced in this book. The implementation and adaptation of XP was not always without its problems but always improved the way we achieved the project. Other XP teams have given a similar assessment.

So far, there are few quantitative measures of the effectiveness of XP, apart from the experiences we have had. The work of Laurie Williams indicates that programming pairs improve the quality of programs. We have surveyed the JWAM framework in various versions through the Technical University of Cottbus, Germany. The results have improved with each JWAM version. This confirms that over several years, XP brings a constant, if not a higher, quality.

Julian Mack has analysed a number of projects and has put forward the hypothesis that projects are often similar to expeditions. In essence, Mack explains this in his PhD thesis by the fact most software projects start with important domain-specific, organisational and technical questions unexplained. The project team has to deal with these questions gradually in the development process. This 'feeling one's way' is similar to the procedure followed for expeditions. In our experience, the expedition metaphor is well suited to XP projects and provides developers with a meaningful starting point when installing XP.

9.2 For those in doubt

Many software developers and managers of development projects are initially sceptical about implementing XP. If you are still uncertain about whether you should implement XP, even after reading the previous chapters, this section is aimed at you.

Managers

XP is not a random process for hackers. The development philosophy behind XP does not solely consist of 'Sit in front of the computer and program'. We have made this clear in each chapter of this book and provided detailed arguments for it. Do not think of XP as an anarchic development process that cannot be planned. It is not.

XP belongs to the group of agile development methods. Have a look at the manifesto of the Agile Alliance (see [AgileAlliance]). We are sure that you will find many basic principles that you would like to implement in your projects. XP is one way of doing this.

We have already described how you could and should implement XP and how you can adapt it to your own project. We can, of course, only base what we have said on our own experience. We can also confirm that XP has been successful in all our projects, which have certainly not been minor. We even create fixed-price XP projects, even though we may have to adapt the process appropriately.

In addition to our own experiences, many other developers, managers and customers have experienced a similar satisfaction in using XP. The community around agile processes in general and XP specifically has grown to a significant extent and the ideas are now well accepted across wide areas of the software engineering community. Agile processes and XP are definitely promising approaches to improving the way we develop high-quality software.

If you are not convinced by these experiences, why not carry out a sample project? Put together a team of 6-8 people, including an experienced XP coach, and give the team a meaningful task. We are convinced that, after just a few weeks, you will be able to judge whether XP is suited to your project or how you can adapt the process. But be careful: frequently, such teams turn out to be hugely more effective and efficient than all other in-house development teams and projects.

Just one more remark: teams often try out XP-like practices and fail; they then claim that XP has not worked. A genuine XP project has to use all the XP practices and put the values and principles into effect. Only then can a team really claim to have used XP. Creating or spreading a false picture of XP does nobody any favours, therefore, do not be taken in by such statements and prevent yourself from making such unsubstantiated assertions. An XP coach can pave the way for XP to work.

Developers

At first, XP is strange for many developers. It was the same for us to start with. Even if we had earlier used parts of XP, some parts were still new and unusual, which is probably the same for you. It is a little peculiar to have your code commented on and changed by others, all of a sudden. Pair programming is also a little weird and you are no longer free to check your e-mails as and when you like. You may wonder whether you would be faster programming alone – but would you? Also, you can no longer make anyone responsible for an error in the program. It was easy, wasn't it, to shift the blame onto a colleague? But have you ever had a problem blamed on you? Has a colleague ever been angry about an error in the program that you have caused?

Get involved in an XP project for just a few weeks. We wouldn't want you to miss this experience. Most of our colleagues (even us) no longer want to program alone. It is a lot easier to have a colleague in the team on hand at any time with whom you can discuss things and with whom you can come to a conclusion. The days that we leave work with an unhappy feeling because a problem was not resolved have sunk to a minimum. It is important that you get really involved with the XP ideas. Being responsible for your own errors and freely voicing your problems are elementary components of an XP project. Without these components, an XP project cannot work.

Provided that you contribute your part to successful team work, you can also enjoy the advantages to the developer of an XP project. Of course, XP projects can also be stressful, at least for a limited period of time. However, this does not mean that the developers are blamed for any failures. And a good XP project does not impose on its developers deadlines that cannot be kept or demand any outcomes that cannot be realised.

In Section 6.3 we described how to become a good XP developer. Take heed of the characteristics that were mentioned there. As a reward, you will work in a friendly, highly motivated and extremely productive environment.

9.3 Outlook

XP is still a new development process. It has a good foundation, but will develop further over the course of time. One important aspect is the fragility of the XP process during the set up. We are convinced that this fragility can be counteracted by suitable artefacts that reify routine activities and therefore stabilise the process. The initial XP artefacts are story cards, task cards and software that supports the integration process (e.g. Integration Server).

9.4 Literature

Agile Alliance. *Agile Manifesto.* http://www.agilealliance.org
XP is an agile process. The Agile Alliance works to retain the foundations of flexible, lightweight software development.

Frequently Asked Questions

In this chapter, we answer the questions that we are asked over and over again about XP. Many of the answers will refer you back to the appropriate place in this book. In this sense, this chapter can be seen almost as a reference index.

Are there any noteworthy projects in which XP has been successfully implemented?

Although XP is relatively new, a number of projects either have been completed or are still running successfully. We have carried out various successful XP projects (see Chapters 1 and 8) and there are a number of other projects around the world.

Can I use XP if I have to carry out a fixed-price project?

XP reflects the conditions of the project practice through a highly cyclical procedure. The aims and functional range are rarely totally clear at the start of the project. It is much more common for the aims and functionality to change during the project. With this in mind, we always argue initially for projects to be carried out on the basis of cost or with a set budget. If the customer insists on a fixed-price project, we first of all carry out a pre-project to clarify the technical requirements (as a rule, this lasts only from a few person days to a few person months). On the basis of the pre-project, we can then quote for the system development as a fixed-price project. Of course, the risk of an incorrect estimation increases with the size of the project. We have carried this out on projects up to US$200,000. If the extent of a project considerably exceeds this, it seems advisable to break it up into several sub-projects.

As a rule, the pre-project produces a prototype or a document that outlines the technical requirements. This gives the customer the security that he can still use the outcome of the pre-project if the subsequent quotation is too expensive. He can use the prototype or the document to provide the contract to another contractor (see Section 5.3).

Does XP work for complex projects?

If the domain-specific background is very complex, the interview techniques, scenarios and glossary (see Section 4.1) should be used. If the political situation is complex (because, for example, the client has different objectives to the user) then it is sensible to split the XP customer role into client and user roles (see Section 3.8). Core systems with construction stages and special systems with project stages (see Section 4.3) are used to show clear rules to all parties if there is political 'confusion'.

Is XP appropriate for long-running projects?

XP also works for long-running projects. In this case, it frequently makes sense to work with a reference architecture, a core system with construction steps, and special systems with project stages.

Is XP appropriate for projects with many developers?

The maximum size of an XP project is not yet fixed. It is however assumed that an XP project cannot cope with much more than 14–16 developers. If many more developers have to be integrated, then it is advisable that you define several projects and form a coordination circle with project representatives.

Does XP work if I do not have any direct customers (e.g. in the case of standard product development, e-business applications, or frameworks)?

In this case, you must find a replacement for the customer (see Chapter 2).

Can XP be used if the project team members have diverse qualifications?

There can be problems if you are working under XP and the developers all have different levels of ability and knowledge. In our experience, there are no problems if the situation is clear to all members of the project and if they all aim to adjust their qualifications to a common level. Pair programming (see Chapter 2) can be very useful for this. For the project manager or coach, it may be sensible in the early stages to assign work explicitly. Guidelines (see Chapter 4) can be used for this assignment and also to maintain an overview.

If XP is changed and extended so much, is it still XP?

This question is of rather theoretical interest to us. What really counts, after all, is the success of the project, and not the name of the method.

Which XP practices can we do without, if we must?

Successful projects can also be carried out without pair programming and metaphors. In our experience, however, productivity is higher if these practices are used. If one of the other practices is not used, it will almost certainly lead to problems in the project (see Chapter 6).

Is it best to introduce the XP practices all at once or one after the other? Which order is best?

XP practices should be introduced cautiously. A possible strategy for the introduction of the practices is described in Chapter 6.

Integrating methods

B

Many companies have existing development methods. In this book, we have made it clear how XP can be adapted. In this chapter, we use examples to show how aspects of other development methods can be integrated with XP. Because of our background, we have used the Tools and Materials approach, however, many of the aspects discussed here should be able to be integrated with other methods.

Metaphors help the developers to communicate with each other about the system and also support a uniform design of the software system. But good metaphors are not always easy to find. Developers are well-advised to acquire as much knowledge as possible about the potential metaphors. They can then better decide on the most suitable metaphors for the incipient development project. In XP, the system architecture is *not* defined first. Nevertheless, it helps the developers if they have some knowledge of architecture. They can quickly recognise when refactorings are necessary in order to keep large systems easy to change. They can bring in tested architectures as background knowledge and thus increase the probability of achieving an architecture that is easy to change.

Against this background, we consider the Tools and Materials approach, with its metaphors and layer architecture, as a *suggestion* for concrete projects and not as a *commandment*. The Tools and Materials approach can be understood as a generic implementation of the metaphor practice. In our projects, we no longer have to look for suitable metaphors, but use the metaphors defined through the Tools and Materials approach such as *material*, *automaton*, *tool* and *service provider*. This uniform choice of metaphors leads to a uniform system architecture that enables developers to quickly get used to projects that are already running. Furthermore, it is relatively easy to see what they have in common with other projects and to abstract them in frameworks (e.g., JWAM).

B.1   The tools and materials approach

Materials, tools, automaton and service providers are the central concepts of interactive application systems, according to the Tools and Materials approach. A *material* carries domain-specific information and is probed and manipulated using *tools*. An application system is thus modelled and implemented as a collection of software materials and tools so that the user can fulfil their tasks depending on the work situation. The software materials should be domain-motivated and should have an identifiable connection with objects that are already present in the workplace. Software tools do not require such a strong connection with the application domain. After all, the way of handling materials in the system should be distinguished from that outside the system, so that the system brings a discernible advantage. The Tools and Materials approach assumes that the essential tasks remain unchanged even after the introduction of the application system. It is therefore important that the tasks are supported optimally by the software tools. Tools are supported in software as they represent the only interface with the user. The user cannot directly probe or manipulate a material in software. He must always use a suitable software tool.

Automata reify tiresome routine tasks. They are set up and started by the user and then deliver a definable result. Physical examples of automata are coffee machines, photocopiers, or cash safes. In application systems, we can distinguish two kinds of automata. Pure software automata share only the concept with physical automata. They function in a similar way to the physical automata but are not connected to them. An example of this kind of automaton is the form copier (which makes a new instance of a blank form, replicating a physical folder holding blank forms). There are also automata that exist physically in the application system and must be connected to it (such as, the cash safe in a bank). In these cases, it makes sense to model the physical automata in the software system. These software system automata are used to find out the state of and to control the physical automata.

The concept of the *service provider* (sometimes called the *domain(-specific) service*) is relatively new in the Tools and Materials approach and therefore is not yet fully known. A service provider supplies a customer with one or more defined services. In the real world, a service provider would be, for example, a taxi driver. In software systems, the service provider concept is used to create a mental connection (a metaphor) between the software system and the application domain. However, we do not transfer the services from the application domain directly into the software system. Thus, a taxi driver does not make sense within software, but a transport mechanism does. Examples of service providers in a software system are the account management system of a bank or the rate calculator in an insurance company.

B.2 The tools and materials layer architecture

The Tools and Materials approach defines a representative micro-architecture for application systems. If the system becomes very large (several thousand classes) a rougher architecture, a macro-architecture, is necessary. The layer architecture depicted in Figure B.1 defines this reference architecture, which we use as a guideline for every large project.

The layer architecture helps to localise concepts and guarantees a certain 'shapeliness' of the system. If the layer architecture is used, developers can assume that a layer does not use higher layers. This helps them to estimate effects and changes more accurately.

Language extensions layer — The *language extensions* make available interfaces and implementations that we would have liked in the programming language. For example, they offer the following services:

- Support for the construction of technical values

- Realisation of the contract model

- Abstractions for automated unit tests (but not the tools for running tests). Initially, it may seem strange to establish higher classes for unit tests, however we can thus equip the elements of the language itself with unit tests.

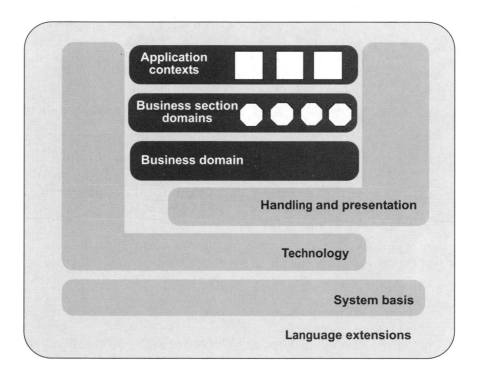

Figure B.1 An example layer architecture from [Züllighoven]

The elements in the base language are completely independent of the application. The features that are implemented and the way in which they are implemented depend on the programming language. The language extensions are used by the layers above.

System basis layer

The *system basis layer* contains the interfaces of the operational (legacy) systems. These systems are encapsulated by 'black box' frameworks and class libraries and are not visible to the layers above. The elements of the system basis layer are completely independent of the application. They can, therefore, be used to construct different interactive application systems. The elements of this layer are used by the layers above (particularly the technology layer). As a rule, Java projects require, at most, one thin system basis layer. The technologies provided by Java are already so close to the desired programming model that they can be added to the technology layer without any problems.

Technology layer

The *technology layer* defines the programming interface through which the upper layers access the technology. The technology layer consists mostly of 'white box' frameworks, which may be supplemented with extensible black box frameworks in order to offer ready-made standard solutions. For example, this layer may contain:

- a connection to a window system that implements the graphical interface for the applications;

- support for communication with other environments or processes, i.e. a common concept of communication.

The elements of this layer can be reused as they are not specific to a particular application. However, it should only provide the technological concepts that are meaningful for the system under development. For example, a networked interactive workstation system requires the support of a window system.

Handling and presentation layer

The *handling and presentation layer* defines the concepts of manipulation and presentation. The fundamental concepts of tool and material are also reified here. For example, the handling and presentation layer includes:

- the environment concept,

- compilation aids (containers, folders, staples) for organising the workplace,

- standard implementations of the design pattern for tools, materials and automatons.

This layer is not tied to a specific application and can therefore be used for all systems that comply with the Tools and Materials approach. If a completely different type of application is developed, perhaps a database application, then this layer is dispensable and may be replaced, for example by a database-specific layer. The handling and presentation layer accesses the technology layer, part of the system basis layer and the language extensions. The components of the handling and presentation layer are used extensively as white box frameworks.

Application-specific layers

The *business domain layer* assembles the basic abstractions of an application. It makes available the technical terms and concepts that determine the textual communication of the remaining system components. As a result, this layer virtually defines the vocabulary for the system components in the application domain.

The *business section domain layer* implements the specific concepts of the application and specifies how to work with them, on the basis of the business domain layer. Normally, the business section domain layer contains the software tools with which the users work. It is divided vertically into product areas that do not directly depend on each other. They use the concepts of the business domain layer in order to communicate with each other. Product ranges can orientate themselves to products, services or business sectors.

The *application context layer* configures the components of the system from the business section layer in order to create the tools for each of the workstations. The components of the application context layer should not depend on each other.

Discussion

We are asked again and again whether the Tools and Materials approach, and the layer architecture in particular, is really compatible with XP. After all, XP is opposed to large preliminary designs. The real question is not whether to use an architecture, but rather how it is formed. The correct use of the architecture is important: each application should have a more or less strongly-defined architecture. A clearly structured architecture makes a system easier to understand and supports changes.

XP understands the architecture as a growing feature. Whenever structural weaknesses are found in the system, refactorings are carried out to eliminate them. Over time, the application gives rise to structures that can be described as the architecture. Our experience is that you can go far with this approach. However, we always have clear goals in mind during refactoring. These goals come from our experience, which has taught us what makes good and bad structures. This experience is enriched with knowledge about the architecture, and the layer architecture introduced here also makes its contribution.

Even if we have an architecture in mind, we do not slavishly stick to it. If appropriate, we may disregard the architecture (either temporarily or permanently). If a requirement cannot be implemented elegantly with an architecture, this is not a problem with the requirement but with the architecture. We often disregard the architecture when implementing requirements; frequently, this violation of the rules turns out to have been only a temporary measure. If the violation continues, it may be the subject of refactoring or it may lead to a redefinition of the architecture.

Conclusion   Our conclusion is that the Tools and Materials approach is very compatible with XP. Architecture ideas borrowed from the Tools and Materials approach always resonate at the back of your mind during the development.

B.3 Literature

Bäumer, D., *et al.* 1996. 'Large Scale Object-Oriented Software-Development in a Banking Environment: An experience report' in Pierre Cointe (ed.), *ECOOP'96 Conference Proceedings*, pp. 73–90. Berlin, Heidelberg, Springer-Verlag.

> *The authors describe a large project in a banking environment that was carried out with Tools and Materials approach.*

Bäumer, D., *et al.* 1997. 'Framework Development for Large Systems' in *Communications of the ACM*, 40(10):52–9.

> *The Tools and Materials approach layer architecture is introduced in this article.*

Bäumer, D., *et al.* 1999. 'Structuring Large Application Frameworks' in Mohamed E. Fayad *et al.* (eds) *Building Application Frameworks: Object-oriented foundations of framework design*, 395–413. New York, Wiley Computer Publishing.

> *The Tools and Materials approach layer architecture is introduced in this article.*

Bürkle, U., Gryczan, G., Züllighoven, H. 1995. 'Object-Oriented System Development in a Banking Project: Methodology, experience, and conclusions' in *Human-Computer Interaction: Empirical Studies of Object-Oriented Design*, 10(2 & 3):293–336. New Jersey, England, Lawrence Erlbaum Associates.

> *Report of the experiences of a Tools and Materials approach project.*

JWAM Framework, IT Workplace Solutions GmbH. http://www.jwam.org
The JWAM framework supports the construction of Tools and Materials approach applications and implements the technical layers of the Tools and Materials approach layer architecture.

Riehle, D., and Züllighoven, H. 1995. 'A Pattern Language for Tool Construction and Integration Based on the Tools and Materials Metaphor' in J.O. Coplien and D.C. Schmidt (eds), *Pattern Languages of Program Design*, pp. 9–42. Reading, Massachusetts, Addison-Wesley.
The Tools and Materials approach construction principles as a collection of patterns.

Züllighoven, Heinz. 2002. *The Object-Oriented Construction Handbook.* to be published by Morgen Kaufmann.
The basis of the Tools and Materials Approach are described in detail in this book. As well as the pure approach, there are also many design instructions and tips for developing software architectures and projects in the object-oriented environment.

Glossary

C

Acceptance test, functional test

Acceptance tests define the criteria that have to be fulfilled to determine that a requirement has been implemented. Acceptance tests are as a rule not formal specifications but are used to define the arrangements between users and developers.

Adaptation

XP has to be adapted to the local conditions and culture of the company.

Assume simplicity, *see* Simplicity

Change, *see also* Incremental change

XP breaks a number of conventional assumptions and many XP practices are unusual. For XP to be successfully implemented, the project team must also embrace the changes that accompany XP. Since the engagement of the project members is vital, a project that forces XP will probably be a failure.

Coach

You cannot transform a conventional project into an XP project simply by giving the members of the project this or another XP book to read. Fundamental aspects of the project culture have to be conveyed and this is done most easily if there is someone in the project who already has experience with XP and is appointed as the XP trainer.

Coding standards

Standardising the source code makes collective ownership easier, for example.

Collective ownership

The whole project team is responsible for the project and the code that is created. Consequently, any member of an XP project may in principle change anything at any time.

Communication, *see also* Open, honest communication

Communication between people is essential for the success of the project. If the communication is no longer effective, this can quickly lead to the failure of the project.

Concrete experiments

During the course of a project, there will be things of which people are (e.g. 'Does the database cater for up to 500 users?'). Practical experiments tackle these issues.

Continuous integration

Developer integrate their changes to the system as quickly and as often as possible.

Courage

Courage is one of the XP values. All members of the project team need courage in order to implement XP and to adopt unusual methods when necessary.

Customer

The customer decides what the developer will program.

Embrace change, *see* Change

eXtreme Programming (XP)

eXtreme Programming is the agile development methodology that is described in this book. XP is based upon four values that can be implemented with twelve practices.

Feedback

When people produce something that affects other people, it is normally difficult to estimate how it will affect those others. Thus, developers can only rarely judge whether a solution meets the requirements of the user. The simplest way of dealing with this problem is to obtain feedback from the people who are affected by the production. Therefore, developers make components of the system that have already been programmed available to the users in order to get feedback from them. Feedback should be given or obtained as quickly as possible. If the time gap between an event and the feedback on this event is too large, the probability that the feedback can be learnt from decreases.

Functional test, *see* **Acceptance test**

Incremental change, *see also* **Changes**

Radical changes always carry a high risk. Therefore, changes should always be carried out incrementally in small steps. If radical changes are necessary, this sometimes indicates that there are problems in the development process. Then, small problems have been discovered so late that they have become large problems.

Measurement

The tracker measures the progress of the project, the quality of the programs, etc. The whole project team should deal honestly with the measurements. All too often, developers ignore the measurements in order not to be responsible for problems in the project.

Metaphor

A metaphor is a representation, an idea of something. The system should be developed alongside a small number of meaningful metaphors that help the project team to develop a common understanding about the behaviour and structure of the application system.

Play to win

All people taking part in the project should 'play to win'. This means that they must have the will and conviction to bring the project to a successful conclusion. If the project team stops playing to win, the project should be ended. If individual project members do not play to win, they should be removed from the team.

On-site customer

There should be an on-site customer or user available to answer questions quickly and easily.

Open, honest communication

XP is based fundamentally on communication. The benefits can however only be gained if people communicate with one another openly and honestly. If problems are covered up, or if any of the people involved work with a hidden agenda, this leads to problems in the project.

Pair programming

When programming in pairs, two developers work on the same computer at the same time. They swap the roles of programmer and reviewer and develop the software together.

Planning game

During the planning game, the customer and the developer determine the requirements that are to be implemented in the next iteration or release. The customer is responsible for prioritisation and the developer for estimation of costs.

Practice

XP defines twelve practices, also called techniques.

Principles

XP has five basic principles: *Rapid feedback, assume simplicity, incremental change, embrace change*, and *quality work*. These principles provide the project members with guidelines for handling the project.

Quality work

Developers want to deliver quality work. In conventional development processes, the quality of the work is frequently sacrificed because of time pressures. This leads, however, to further delays in the development and to frustrated developers. XP takes into account the fact that the developers want to deliver quality work and that poor quality quickly leads to a delay in the development. In XP, therefore, if there are difficulties with meeting the deadline, it is not the quality that is reduced but the functionality. The user gets more from a correct implementation of the most important functions than from a faulty implementation of all functions.

Rapid feedback, *see* Feedback

Refactoring

Refactoring describes the restructuring of a system whilst keeping its functionality. After a refactoring, all acceptance tests that were satisfied before the refactoring must again be run successfully.

Responsibility

In XP, responsibility is not allocated, but taken on by the members of the team. For example, the developers estimate the requirements and thereby take on responsibility for the estimation. In conventional development processes, the estimation is frequently carried out by the project manager though the developers then are responsible for completing the work within the assigned time.

Role

XP defines a number of roles for the project. These roles can be allocated in different ways to the people in the project.

Simple design

The system should have a simple design. If it has a simple design it can be developed quickly, understood easily, and further developed effectively.

Simplicity

Simplicity is one of the central XP values that is used throughout the project: program design, communication channels, project plans, etc. If there are several possible solutions to a problem, it is not always easy to decide which is the simplest solution. These kinds of decisions are part of the learning process. The project team must be aware that perfection (the simplest possible solution) is not always achieved but can always be striven for.

Small releases

Small extensions of the system that have been developed should be delivered. The users can profit from the continuous development at a very early stage and faulty developments can be recognised quickly.

Small initial investment

The investments should pay off as quickly as possible. We cannot be sure how the world will be tomorrow, next week, or next year. High investments are always a big risk because we cannot be sure whether they will pay off or not.

Teach how to learn

An essential element of XP is its flexibility to adjust to changed boundary conditions. To be able to use this flexibility, the project team has to be able to learn quickly new requirements, technologies, and so on. For most developers, this means initially that they have to learn how to teach. The XP coach is responsible for teaching how to learn.

Technique

XP defines twelve techniques, or practices.

Testing

XP systems should always be well protected by unit tests and acceptance tests.

'The simplest thing that could possibly work'

You should always choose the simplest solution that can work to guarantee that the product is produced with the lowest cost.

Tracker

The tracker monitors the development process. The tracker takes samples from defined places in the development process and feeds the findings back into the process.

Travel light

The flexibility of XP is based on the lightweight development process. The 'travel light' metaphor is perfectly suited to this context.

Unit test

Developers test their classes with unit tests, also called module tests. Unit tests should cover most of the system and should be executed regularly.

Values

XP is based on four simple values: *communication*, *simplicity*, *feedback* and *courage*. Once the project team internalises these values, the rest follows.

Work with people's instincts, not against them

The instincts of the team should be used. Frequently, members of the project instinctively know if the project is going in the wrong direction. This should be taken into account. On the other hand, developers who have worked in conventional projects for a long time may develop instincts that are no longer adequate for an XP project. For example, these developers may instinctively try to create a complete data model, which clearly contradicts the XP values.

Index